3

15. Knowledge Management System Operation...........187

16. Conclusion 196

Bibliographic References 197

About the author...............................200

Acknowledgments

To my beloved and marvelous wife and my son, who fills me with great pride.

To the good fortune of having had a mother who was a teacher and a father who always believed in the value of education.

To the privilege of having sufficient health and knowledge to write my second book.

KCS is a service mark of the Consortium for Service Innovation

A note on terminology

Each industry or line of business has its own terminology. As we are dealing with help desk and customer care in this book, some terminology conflicts may arise. In help desk, the person who handles customer problems, requests or inquiries is most times called agent or technician. In customer care, those persons are called agents or customer service representatives.

The terms suggested by KCS, according to its glossary, are:

Requestor	A knowledge worker seeking information or resolution to an issue.
Responder	A knowledge worker providing a resolution to an issue or assisting in the development of a resolution to an issue.

"Responder", therefore, may apply to agent, technician or customer service representative.

"Requestor" may apply to the user or client requesting a service or with a problem or issue to be solved.

About this Book

This book is divided into two parts.

In its first part, it presents conceptual core definitions of knowledge management, with a theoretical basis and synthesis arising from research made in several publications, among books, articles, white papers and blogs. The result of this work is a summary of huge material, facilitating the introduction to the subject and understanding thereof.

The focus of the book, however, is not restricted to knowledge management in itself. It is not a work which exhausts the subject, although it is a good reference for those wishing to be introduced to the issue.

The objective is to present a practical proposition for development of initiatives of knowledge management applied to help desk and customer-care. To achieve this, the first part of the book also presents concepts of KCS (Knowledge-Centered Service), a set of practices and a specific methodology focused upon technical support, to improve the efficacy of resolving problems. KCS, however, is not limited merely to solving problems, being able to be adapted to handling requests in general.

KCS is the result of compiling best practices and discussing initiatives by a group of large information technology companies, which formed a consortium to share ideas and experiences.

The areas of technical support, whether in help desk or in customer care, depend upon the qualification of the people involved in the process, and this in turn depends upon knowledge.

Indeed, how can one resolve a problem without knowing the subject concerned? The worst is that such subject is usually a technical issue, or is related to something technical, as the functioning of software or a product. Even in the cases of requisitions, where the agent does not go to resolve a problem, but to render a service to handle a request, knowledge is required: how to proceed to fulfill the necessity, or to whom and how forward the requisition, and what information is necessary? And if the requisition is a request for information, where to search for this information to pass to the requestor?

KCS was created, with certain assumptions common to knowledge management, to deal with obtaining, sharing and transmitting knowledge to improve service, involving incidents and problems. As the methodology itself determines, it can be adapted to aid in forming a useful knowledge basis for handling requisitions.

In the first part of the book KCS is presented and commented upon in a detailed manner, including its concepts, objectives and practices.

As the theoretical concepts are presented and explained, and that, therefore, a context is provided, in its **second part** the book develops and presents a practical proposal of planning and implementing a knowledge management system using the practices of KCS.

What is being proposed is the use of the conceptual basis of KCS, but not being limited thereto.

Indeed, a roadmap resulting from the concepts as well as the experience and a certain creative boldness of this author is presented.

The model proposed is something practical and applicable in companies of any size which have areas of technical support, service-desk, shared services or customer care. As they are practices suggested, they can be adapted, obviously, but their structure has a composition which allows the understanding of the themes in a logical and clear sequence, without ever losing sight of the essential academic concepts of knowledge management and KCS, obviously.

Introduction

"Knowledge, in the current age, is a perishable product" The author

Nobody's born knowing

After thinking a lot about an effective phrase related to the theme to begin the book, I arrived at this one. It is short, direct and probably all the readers have already heard it at least once in their life. What exactly does this phrase have to do with the book? It is a rhetorical question, clearly, as it has everything to do with it.

As human beings, we are born without knowing anything, only with certain primitive instincts.

After a very short time alive, we begin to learn. First with the mother, then with the father, with the family. We continue learning through our observation of the world, with sensory experience of positive and negative stimuli, and then with socialization, through siblings or friends. Until one day a more formal learning begins, at school.

From our birth, learning never stops.

All this occurs with all of us as individuals. As a collectivity, in the case, as a species, as human beings, we also learn. And how! It is only due to our collective learning that we still exist. That is how we have managed to perpetuate ourselves. Clearly, any reader may already be thinking that, as a species, we not all that clever, as we are destroying our planet, finishing with our resources, etc., etc. We shall not enter into judging values, only accept that collectively we have learnt a lot and this makes us evolve.

First, in the dawn of humanity, we learnt how to gather and hunt better, and then we learnt that it would be better to establish ourselves, thanks to the knowledge regarding the cultivation of plantations; we obtained important knowledge to protect and shelter ourselves against the weather and also to face enemies. Later, we began to learn sciences and did not stop thereafter. It is not irrational to think that without knowledge nowadays we would not be able to produce sufficient food for all humanity.

Going to another line of reasoning, I propose a pause for a quick reflection, something which I have been thinking about for some time. Imagine if we could measure the accrued knowledge that each current product contains. We would arrive at incredibly large and absurd quantities or values.

Explaining better, let us take as an example any product which is part of our lives nowadays. Something common and simple, such as the television. The quantity of accrued knowledge so that the simple act of watching television is possible is unimaginable. We can begin with electricity, in the imagination or inspiration and afterwards in the study and experimentation required to arrive at its invention; next in the improvement of its distribution. In this same line of thought, we had valves and transistors, then chips. Transmission of radio waves which led to the transmission of images. Technology of recording, first of voice and afterwards also of images. Join together all this knowledge and today we can watch television...

Thus, would all and any learning have had any value if it had not been transmitted from individual to individual, group to group, generation to generation? Individuals are not eternal, but humanity has perpetuated itself, and goes beyond the individual duration of people. Therefore, it cannot be denied that transmitting knowledge and perpetuating it is as important as obtaining it. Do you, the reader, agree?

I believe that everything so far makes sense. But as this is not a book about anthropology or sociology, we have to deal with companies and business.

And we can think about companies in practically the same way as about individuals, in this context of learning and knowledge. Why?

Well, because companies also learn. And they only survive and perpetuate themselves if they learn and transmit their knowledge. If we regard a company as a being, albeit an imaginary collective being, but which does not cease to be a being, it is reasonable to think that companies learn. And they perpetuate their knowledge, as they extrapolate the duration of individuals. They create a type of collective knowledge to the extent that they develop, evolve, react to threats and difficulties, indeed, evolve in their lives.

***

To leave the area of digressions, let us take some practical examples of how, or what, companies learn. Some of this learning is well-known and even commonplace. Who has not seen, heard or at can at least imagine one of the following examples?

- "We've stopped selling to that region, there's no profit...".
- "To not depend upon market oscillations, we begin to export...".
- "We've changed the contract services package because...".

Any one of the sentences exemplified above constitutes entrepreneurial learning. Or lessons learnt.

Perhaps, in small companies, they represent decisions taken by the owners themselves or directors, as a result of their direct observations and conclusions, their personal learning. There are cases where the managers are able to follow up practically all the areas and operations almost personally. To the extent that companies are larger, the greater the likelihood that top management is unable to follow up operations and areas personally – it does not manage to be omnipresent. It tends to delegate to hierarchical levels, and the decisions inevitably come to be taken based upon data and information.

What is certain is that companies really learn and grow with the learning, like people do. But they only learn through people. And they depend upon people to share and transmit knowledge.

Thus, taking another step in the direction of the focus of this book, what is knowledge management and what is it for?

First, it has to be concluded that companies which are successful learn something useful. Those which do not survive probably did not perceive the importance of applying the learning.

Staying with the case of the companies which learn, the value of the learning and knowledge is unquestionable. One of the main, if not the main objective of knowledge management, is to make this learning systematic and transmitted in the most varied areas and hierarchical levels of the organization. Knowledge management recognizes the importance of the knowledge of people, individually, as a very great value of the companies; so great that it is called "intellectual asset" or "knowledge asset".

The key point of knowledge management is to identify, obtain, store, transmit and maintain updated this knowledge, making it available and above all useful for the majority of the people in the organization, in accordance with its relevance to each area of activity. All this in a systematic manner, i.e., so that it is done in an automatic and cyclical way.

There subtly arose another point here which deserves emphasizing: the expression "maintain updated", related to knowledge. At the time in which we live, when everything evolves increasingly quickly, knowledge becomes obsolete at a ridiculous rate. Knowledge, nowadays, is a perishable product. So, the update is as essential as its identification, obtaining and storage.

"Knowledge without update tends to become trash".

A real and everyday fact in practically all companies cannot be ignored: namely, that knowledge, being in individuals, goes away with them, if they leave the organization.

Furthermore, individuals have vacations and fall ill, and it is not ideal that the company depends upon the availability of a certain person to operate well. Who has not known a company where they say things like "we're going to have to call Such-and-Such in his vacation, as only he knows how to do such a thing"?

With knowledge management, one of the various results which can be expected is that this knowledge of high value of individuals is systematically shared and, therefore, more within the reach of the organization. At first perhaps, and indeed probably, this Such-and-Such of the example will not be willing to share his vital information. He may feel threatened at losing prestige and importance, and this is natural. It happens in many cases.

Knowledge management acknowledges these human factors and is also concerned about how to deal with them.

First Part

Concepts and Foundations of Knowledge Management and KCS

1. Knowledge Management

We have already looked, in the introduction, at certain reflections relevant to knowledge and its importance in our age. Much more could be said or written, concerning reflections and conjectures about knowledge.

In this chapter we are going to look, in a more pragmatic way, at the main concepts of knowledge management, at least the basic ones for developing the work proposed herein, which is that of planning and implementing a knowledge management system applied to help desk and customer care. We are not going to get caught up in or describe the history and evolution of knowledge management, or enter into concepts of epistemology, not because we do not consider them important, but to be focused upon presenting items more relevant to our purpose in a practical way.

The availability of literature related to the issue is huge, with different views, lines of thought and approaches. It is important to bear in mind, once more, that this book does not intend to explore deeply and exhaust the subject knowledge management in itself, but to use it as a conceptual basis to construct a practical method which supports efficaciously the process of attending to users and customers. If the reader is interested in the issue and wishes to know it in depth, there is a lot of literature available which develops the concepts.

1.1. Definition

As it could not be otherwise, one cannot begin to look at any subject without defining knowledge management. And, incredible though it seems, this is a really complex task. Complex why? Because there is no single definition universally accepted, or sole and standardized. According to Kimiz Dalkir (2005), an informal study which he made indicated more than one hundred different definitions published, more than 70 of them being considered to be good definitions!

I confess that I worried about transcribing here dozens of different definitions, because I do not consider, personally, the formal definitions of many different authors as essential as developing the work proposed herein. What really matters, in my opinion, are some key words and certain basic concepts which are highlighted in these definitions.

I propose that we look at a formal definition, translated and adapted from the glossary of knowledge management (Knowledge Research Institute):

"**Knowledge management** is the *systematic, explicit and deliberate construction, application and update of knowledge to maximize the efficacy related to the knowledge of companies and the* return from the knowledge and assets of intellectual capital. It encompasses deliberate and systematic analysis, synthesis, evaluation and implementation of changes related to knowledge to attain objectives and ensure that activities related to knowledge management are executed appropriately and attain their objectives".

Although this definition seems, at first sight, complex – and, I admit, I consider the phrases really a little long – that which is most important is removing from it the most determining key concepts. With them, the understanding of what knowledge management and its objectives is will be much clearer.

So, we shall do that. We are going to decompose the most important key concepts of knowledge management, in accordance with the previous definitions, to then analyze them.

The passage "systematic, explicit and deliberate construction, application and update of knowledge to maximize the efficacy related to the knowledge of companies" clearly denotes that knowledge management is a continuous process, and the key words for it are construction, application and update – the cycle encompasses these three aspects continually.

The terms "systematic, explicit and deliberate" deserve special attention, as they reinforce that knowledge management is not an isolated and separate initiative. Furthermore, it must be clear, exposed, disclosed and executed by own deliberation, initiative and will.

Continuing the analysis, regarding the passage "encompasses deliberate and systematic analysis, synthesis, evaluation and implementation of changes related to knowledge" we can deduce that the main point here is related to the changes. Knowledge management requires changes, in the organization and in people. It is important to stress that the word 'systematic' appears again.

Finally, but no less important, it is worth pointing out that intellectual capital assets are mentioned, which will be detailed further on in this work.

Returning to the trinomial 'construction, application and update' of knowledge, we could also understand the concept with another definition of knowledge management, more synthetic, used by several authors:

Capture, organization, storage, transmission and update of knowledge.

One feature of knowledge management which needs to be emphasized, in its conception and classical definitions, concerns its multidisciplinary nature.

It is related to several fields of science, as cognitive science, linguistics, taxonomy, archival science, anthropology, journalism, technical writing, etc.

In practice, whatever the definition, knowledge management is concerned with this set of items emphasized – and, obviously, always doing this in a systematic and deliberate manner. However many definitions we seek, we shall probably never move away from these concepts. The definitions can be more oriented towards business, scientific or academic. It is certain that they all revolve around this.

It should be highlighted once more, as already mentioned previously, that there is a vast number of points of view concerning definitions, objectives and scope. Perhaps the most radical form of definition that certain authors use is that knowledge management has no formal definition. There are even those who assert that it refers to a passing fashion, as in the case of Wilson (2002), who states that knowledge cannot be managed and that, at most, it is possible to have practices of sharing knowledge.

1.2. Core concepts

For the sequence of our objective, it is important that certain core concepts are understood, because they will be used throughout our planning and implementation of a knowledge management system. They are presented below.

- Data. Generally speaking, it can be stated that it is any content which can be observed. It can be a fact, a measurement, a statistic.

- Information. It is a content which represents analyzed data, thereby gaining context. This is the fundamental differentiation, the context representing a meaning.

- Knowledge. In a simpler manner, it can be stated that it represents the understanding of information. The formal definition of knowledge is perhaps broader than that of knowledge management itself. There are several currents of thought which are concerned with trying to give a definition for knowledge, as, for example, epistemology. Concerning our objective, in a pragmatic manner, we can adopt 'the understanding of information'.

Several authors seek to give examples to try to make clearer these definitions of data, information and knowledge. Let us look at two examples.

According to Kimiz Dalkir (2005):

- Data: programming of films shown in cinemas.

- Information: I cannot leave the office before 05pm, so I will go to the session of 07pm in a cinema near where I work.
- Knowledge: at this time, it will be difficult to park. It is better to go by train. Anyway, I will buy the ticket by the Internet to avoid queues at the last moment...

While in accordance with the example of Bellinger (2004):

- Data: number 100 or simply 5%.
- Information: with context related to a bank account, the 5% can become interest rate and 100 can represent balance in account, in the case $ 100.00.
- Knowledge: if $ 100.00 is applied in an investment which remunerates 5%, then it is known that at the end of the period the balance will be $ 105.00.

Several other examples are given by other authors. I believe that the two mentioned allow a better understanding of the concepts.

1.3. Knowledge types

This concept is one of the most important and perhaps one of the most mentioned and used in all the literature of knowledge management. There are two types of knowledge:

- Tacit. Tacit knowledge is everything which is not documented formally. It is in people's heads, being equivalent to the knowledge which people hold. It is personal, at the level of individuals.

- Explicit. Explicit knowledge, as opposed to tacit knowledge, is everything which is formally documented, stored, written, recorded, indeed, it is in another place besides people's heads. It can be in the form of documents, systems, reports, sites, posts, etc. Generally speaking, it can be stated that, depending upon the knowledge type, its importance and context of use, it is desirable to transform tacit knowledge into explicit knowledge.

There is unanimity among practically all the authors that, in companies, tacit knowledge is proportionally much greater than explicit knowledge. Many use the analogy of the iceberg, in that the tip which is exposed, out of the water, represents the explicit knowledge in companies, while the submerged part, immensely larger, is the tacit knowledge. Oddly enough, the only difference of opinion among them is regarding the size of the percentage which corresponds to tacit and explicit knowledge.

Having understood these concepts, it is natural to note that, for companies, explicit knowledge is much more desirable than tacit knowledge, for several reasons, mainly related to retaining and sharing the knowledge. Explicit knowledge facilitates sharing, without depending upon individuals, from the point of view of executing entrepreneurial processes. Once more I take the liberty of commenting that, if we went deeply into knowledge management, we would see that there are definitions of different types of tacit knowledge and that not all of them are liable to becoming explicit, but, regarding the knowledge that people hold which is necessary for executing business processes, this definition is not so important.

Many authors defend the notion that the objective of knowledge management is not only to seek the migration of tacit knowledge to explicit knowledge, but this is, undoubtedly, one of the greatest ones. As our focus is not upon knowledge management as a whole, we can consider this approach satisfactory.

1.4. Knowledge conversion processes

We have already concluded that it is desirable to transform tacit knowledge which is relevant into explicit knowledge, when this is applicable.

So, we can try to understand the ways which exist for this conversion.

Means were defined by which knowledge is transformed from tacit to explicit, explicit to tacit, and so on. As referred to in KMKnowledge.com, the publication "The Knowledge-Creating Company: how Japanese companies create the dynamics of innovation", of Ikujior Nonaka and Hirotaka Takeuchi (1995), defined the following forms of converting knowledge:

Table 1.1. Knowledge conversion

	To tacit	To explicit
From tacit	Socialization (1)	Externalization (2)
From explicit	Internalization (3)	Combination (4)

(1) It corresponds to the interpersonal relationship, where people communicate and exchange knowledge, formally and informally.

(2) It corresponds to the process of documenting the knowledge which is in people's heads.

(3) It can be seen as learning, when we indicate and study recorded contents and internalize knowledge. Reading this book, for example, can be considered to be a form of internalization.

(4) It corresponds to a situation where recorded contents are used to compose others. As an example, one can mention a case of engineering project where several specifications from different areas are documented and afterwards added to other incremental documentation.

Nonaka and Takeuchi (1995) describe that the creation of knowledge consists of a social process between individuals where the transformations are not one-way, but interactive and spiral shaped, which was known in the relevant literature as "spiral of knowledge".

1.5. Knowledge and information assets

So far, I have repeatedly defended the value and importance of knowledge.

I believe that at this stage no doubt remains concerning this. It is so true that, according to knowledge management, information and knowledge are considered to be assets themselves. That is right, assets, like property and accounting assets of companies.

Indeed, already in 1994 Peter Drucker was a pioneer when he wrote that he believed that "the value of organizations would not lie in capital, natural resources or work, but in knowledge". Since then the concept has been gaining followers so that, currently, it is no longer questioned. The sole novelty is regarding the name by which these assets of information and knowledge are known, as many call them the intellectual capital of companies. Certain authors refer to this as intangible assets. Whatever the name, in our case it is important to focus upon the concept of knowledge assets.

Knowledge assets are part of the intangible assets which refer to knowledge, such as "know-how", best practices, intellectual property, etc.

Knowledge assets can be divided into human (people, teams, communities), structural (processes and procedures) and technological (technologies which handle the sharing of knowledge).

In other words, we can state that knowledge assets can be represented by the tacit knowledge and explicit knowledge of organizations.

In certain cases, we can also use the name information assets.

Some examples of information assets in companies are processes, procedures, management systems, reports, emails, spreadsheets, etc.

We are going to work quite a lot with the concept of information assets. We shall see further on their identification, analysis and planning for obtaining, storing and transmitting them.

1.6. Knowledge mapping

Now that we know that organizations have knowledge assets, and we have defined what they are, a crucial question which arises is:

How to identify knowledge assets?

Within knowledge management, mapping is a process which aims to determine what knowledge assets are and where they are in organizations, as well as the flow of information and the relationship of the knowledge holders with each other and with the processes in which they take part. It is also advisable to identify the criticality of the assets related to the processes and the dependency which people have of them.

The result of a work of mapping knowledge is a type of inventory of what the company knows, the information which it has, be it tacit or explicit, as well as who knows what – exactly in this way, related to individuals –, which people have knowledge necessary for executing processes.

The mapping is absolutely fundamental for analyzing which information and knowledge are critical in organizations and what the dependency is between people and processes. This means, in other words, determining which people the processes depend upon and what knowledge the people depend upon to execute the processes. It is the basis for work of planning for the transformation of tacit knowledge into explicit knowledge.

Knowledge mapping means determining which people the processes depend upon and what knowledge the people depend upon to execute the processes.

Beginning to map knowledge may appear, at first sight, complex, given the volume of information in an organization. It is advisable, therefore, that the mapping is done by process. Once a process has been chosen, it is suggested that the following information is studied:

- Knowledge desirable and necessary for the process. It may be concluded, in this study, that certain desirable information or knowledge does not exist. It is a good opportunity to evaluate what there is and what is desired or required.
- Functions of the people who take part in the process (roles exercised or attributions).
- Explicit information assets.
- Tacit information assets.
- Criticality of these assets.
- Information lacking (knowledge gaps).

1.7. Proactive and reactive management

The knowledge mapping will establish a balance sheet of assets which exist in organizations and their classification as to whether they are explicit or tacit, as well as to their criticality. It will also determine a possible "negative balance" of knowledge, in the case of shortage being detected, or also the need to transform tacit knowledge into explicit knowledge. Regarding explicit assets, it is important to analyze their quality. This process as a whole can be defined as proactive management, as it seeks to analyze the availability and quality of the assets and determine which ones do not yet exist, but are necessary.

While reactive management is concerned with creating assets, or knowledge, as they are necessary, upon demand. The concept may perhaps appear strange at first analysis, as the question which seems to leap to one's eyes is: why not do everything proactively and avoid having to be reactive? The quality and management techniques usually focus greatly upon this aspect: planning and executing in advance.

The truth is that, especially when dealing with help desk and customer care processes, which are the focus of this work, there can be advantages and disadvantages in both approaches.

Below, we list some of them.

Proactive knowledge management

Advantages:

- Knowledge available and validated before being required.

Disadvantages:

- Cost can be high, as there may be generation of contents little or never used.
- It may not be efficacious, as it is based upon the view of engineers, analysts or agents, and not of users or customers – more adherent in the case of attending to customers and users.

Reactive knowledge management

Obtaining knowledge at the moment that there is the demand, i.e., when agents are in contact with requestors.

Advantages:

- Cost potentially less (it is only documented in accordance with requirements), avoiding the creation of knowledge which may never be used.
- Knowledge created as part of the process and immediately available.
- It obtains the context of the customer's requirement.
- Reuse of solutions.

Disadvantages:

- Not available upon the first occurrence.
- Quality of the documentation may be impaired, as it is not done by specialists in writing or structuring information.
- It can generate inaccuracies.
- It can generate redundancy.

Note

The KCS methodology is based fundamentally upon the concept of reactive knowledge generation, which will be looked at in detail further on in this book.

1.8. Strategic alignment of knowledge management

Above all, we are going to bear in mind that one of the great differentiation factors of companies, nowadays, is their intellectual capital. We can conclude that, to generate intellectual capital, efficacious and systematic knowledge management is required.

To exemplify, and make it clearer, the intellectual capital of companies can be imbedded in or be part of market positioning, patents, technologies, cutting edge products or services, management capacity, processes, indeed, everything which a company does or presents with excellence.

Due to its importance and the impact which changes can cause in organizations, knowledge management must be aligned with the strategic planning of companies, more precisely with the competitive strategy adopted by them.

As per the portal Business Wisdom, referred to in the work "The Discipline of Market Leaders", of Treacy and Wiersema, there are three fundamental differentiating strategies which companies can adopt:

- relationship and intimacy with customers;
- leadership in products or services;
- operational excellency.

Below I present some of the possible strategic alignments which can be executed for knowledge management, for each one of these orientations:

- **Competitive strategy of leadership in products or services**. Use of knowledge management for the continuous development and improvement of products and services, including feedback of market, customer and consumer, technical documentation, R&D,

projects and lessons learnt. The collaborative construction of knowledge is used to produce better products or services.

- **Competitive strategy of relationship and intimacy with customers**. Knowledge management in favor of knowing more and better the customers and their requirements, aiding in defining products and services oriented towards market demands. It can also be concerned with creating products and services in order to generate added value for customer business. In this case, important and critical knowledge assets would be information related to customers and their market, updated mainly by the commercial area and consumed by the other areas, such as marketing and product development.

- **Competitive strategy of operational excellency**. In this area, knowledge management can aid in improving processes, from their definition, including execution and continuous improvement, as well as in cost control and reduction.

Choo (1998) developed a theoretical model in which he states that knowledge organization makes strategic use of information in three different ways, summarized as follows:

- Sensemaking, allowing an understanding of what the organization is and what it does. This item is more related to the strategy, including definition of business and declaration of vision, besides positioning and strategic objectives.
- Creation of knowledge, more related to the focus which we are dealing with in this book. It is related to

33

obtaining, organizing and sharing knowledge, allowing the development of new skills and capacities and using them in creating or improving products or services.

- Decision-making, related to the decision-making process in general.

We are still far, very far, from exhausting the concepts and theories of knowledge management. I sought to synthesize and present the main and most basic concepts, so that they can aid in understanding the following topics.

Let us go now to a methodology, based upon knowledge management, oriented towards IT technical support and help desk, known by the acronym KCS – Knowledge-Centered Service.

2. KCS – Knowledge-Centered Support

2.1. Introduction

KCS is a methodology based upon practices which was created by a non-profit alliance of service and support organizations called Consortium for Service Innovation™ (CSI), formed by technology companies which render support services to customers and users, with the main objective of resolving challenges common to this type of service – specifically planning and sharing best practices of obtaining, structuring and reusing knowledge.

It began to be developed as of 1992, and currently is in version 6. At the moment, some of the members of the alliance are Cisco, HP, BMC, Dell, Oracle and Salesforce.

The objective of this book is not to transcribe and reproduce all the KCS methodology. We are going to present its structure and key points, commenting upon them in the most didactic manner possible. At various points, I present my free interpretation of the concepts, with adaptations of context. I recognize the copyright of CSI and the property of the brand KCS. The contents referred to are duly credited in the bibliographical reference section. I believe that I am contributing to the disclosure of ideas and practices to a larger audience.

In this chapter a conceptual basis is established to then, next, in the second part of the book, present the proposition of a roadmap of planning and implementation of knowledge management based upon concepts of own knowledge management and practices of KCS.

KCS – Knowledge-Centered Service

All the methodology of KCS, with its practices, is defined in what is called "Practices Guide". There is also another complementary contents, called "Principles and core concepts" and "Adoption Guide". These contents are available on the consortium site, at www.serviceinnovation.org/kcs.

Important note

KCS is the service mark of the Consortium for Service Innovation™. To simplify the writing, in this book the symbols SM and TM are omitted, which does not imply the lack of acknowledgment of brand rights.

2.2. Definition

KCS is a methodology which can be best defined by the four fundamental precepts which it presents:

- Creation of knowledge content as byproduct of the solution of requirements.
- Evolution of content based upon demand and use.
- Development of knowledge base resulting from collective experience and collaboration.
- Acknowledgement by learning, collaboration, sharing and improvement.

2.3. Challenges, perceptions and requirements

The motivating factors and challenges which led companies to organize themselves and define practices as those of KCS do not differ from those observed in companies of different sizes and business areas.

In your company, dear reader, are the following items part of your reality or not?

- Budgetary reduction.
- Increased technological complexity.
- Growing costs.
- Increased demand.

It can be stated that, due to the aforesaid factors, related to their service centers, companies wish to:

- Reduce costs.
- Escalate scope and quality of services.
- Qualify professionals.

Common perceptions were detected in the companies taking part in the consortium. These perceptions of the different stakeholders, once compiled, showed the following trends:

Table 2.1. Main perceptions of services by stakeholder

Stakeholder	Perception
Client **(users)**	Lack of confidence, perception that support doesn't solve issues or take so much time to solve them, etc

Technicians (agentes, responders)	Unable to fulfill user's needs, high complexity, low reward and recognition "users are always dissatisfied, Always want solutions right now", etc
Company	-Users are not satisfied -Clients requirements always higher -Pressure for cost reduction

Is the scenario described, as a whole or in part, related to your reality?

If any of these points concern you, I believe that it is worth your while to continue reading.

2.4. Benefits expected

Any system, practice or methodology which is implemented in an organization can have different results from those obtained in another one. This is because there is a myriad of factors which can affect the performance and the result, whether related to resources made available, time of dedication and commitment and qualification of the people. The results obtained also depend upon the maturity level of the system, obviously.

In CSI consortium, the participants present and discuss their results. The most useful aspect of this is being able to take certain results as a benchmark. As reported in the KCS practices guide, the participants obtained satisfactory results concerning the reduced time in resolving incidents, training of new coworkers, user or customer satisfaction and support coworker satisfaction.

There are three categories of benefits:

- Operational efficiency
- Self-service success
- Organizational learning and improvement

Certain figures which the participants and consortium disclose are as follows:

Quicker solution of incidents and requisitions:

- 50%-60% resolution time reduction.
- 30%-50% increased resolution at first contact.

Optimization in the use of resources:

- 70% improvement in the time required to enable new coworkers for work.
- 20%-35% increased retention of people.
- 20%-40% increased coworker satisfaction.

Implementation of electronic services:

- Improved success in using self-help by users and customers.
- Up to 50% customer adhesion to self-help.

Organizational learning:

- Availability of useful information for product development.
- Reduction of 10% of incidents by eliminating causes.

Very good, is it not?

For those extremely interested with return, the (in)famous ROI, there are some important figures that can be sought and, which, therefore, can enable a calculation of return on investment.

To the skeptical, those who may be thinking "This is a dream, I want to see it in practice... in my company things do not work like that...", I can only say that the practices and method make sense and in many places function.

In this book, we are presenting a practical roadmap which is worth at least trying.

If it is not implemented successfully in everything, part of it may help at some level of improvement. We are going to recall that in the definition of knowledge management there appeared a key concept which is that of change. Here, exactly the same concept applies. The company needs to change. Change your mentality and your beliefs.

For most organizations, adoption of KCS represents a major transformation.

Indeed, what does it cost to believe and try?

2.5. Concepts

We are going to revisit here certain concepts which were already mentioned in the previous chapter.

I am going to describe them here according to the point of view of KCS, as defined in its glossary.

- Data: Words or numbers not organized.
- Information: Organized data, but without utility.

- Knowledge: Information with utility, context and experience associated with its use. Information is transformed into knowledge at the moment of its use, obtained by interaction and experience.
- Knowledge base: Technology mounted for storage and recovery of knowledge.

An important concept, according to KCS, is that **knowledge is constantly changing, is never 100% correct and never 100% complete**, always **having to be validated by use** and **obtained by interaction and experience**.

Knowledge assets

According to KCS, there are four types of knowledge assets:

- **Articles**. They are the knowledge base contents, the base records. Represent the collective experience of the support organization in solving problems and answering questions and may include different issues, as usage or "how to" for instance. Articles integrate the perspective of three parts: requestors, responders and company.
- **People profiles**. The people, in this case, are all those involved in rendering support services. The profiles can include knowledge and qualification of people.
- **Account profiles**. Useful information about the customer, its business and, in many cases, concerning the relationship of the customer with the service provider.

41

- **Customer configuration**. Configuration related to the technological operational environment, and everything which is relevant and useful to aid in handling and solving problems.

2.6. KCS and ITIL

Before advancing in the concepts and understanding of KCS, it is appropriate to evaluate the ITIL library, as many organizations adopt its practices to a greater or lesser extent. For those in this situation, certain questions may be arising regarding KCS. The questions which we shall seek to answer in this topic are as follows:

- Does KCS overlap ITIL or complement it?
- How can both be used?
- What are the benefits?

First, it is important to contextualize and from there make the comparison. It is probable that the great majority of readers already know ITIL, but even so we are going to revise the concepts in order to establish the comparison and analyze the feasibility and justification of coexistence. I take advantage of it to highlight the key points of comparison together with the concepts, as below.

ITIL is a library which supplies guidelines to service providers, including related functions and processes, to offer quality. It is the model (framework) most renowned for a set of practices and seeks the alignment of the IT services with business requirements. The main concern of

ITIL is with the quality of the services made available by IT to users.

ITIL organizes its processes in five life cycle phases: services strategy, services design, services transition, services, operation and continuous service improvement.

KCS is a model (framework) and a methodology. It offers detailed guidelines for obtaining, structuring, reusing and improving articles of knowledge to aid in the efficiency and efficacy of the services rendered. It is based upon a dual loop process, which is also cyclical and seeks continuous improvement – we shall see further on, in detail, these processes.

One conclusion which can be drawn from an analysis of the concepts is that ITIL is more encompassing, oriented towards the services offered by IT by service providers, and aligned with business requirements. KCS, in turn, is oriented towards the generation and maintenance of knowledge to support the rendering of services. It is, therefore, focused upon knowledge management.

Thus, it can be stated that, without the shadow of a doubt, KCS is ideal to complement ITIL. Both can benefit from each other.

As ITIL is a guide, it does not determine how the things must be done, it only recommends that the things are done. It is plausible and perfectly acceptable to think of using the concepts of KCS complementing processes and functions of ITIL.

An area which may perhaps lead to many questions is regarding the Knowledge Management process, of ITIL, which is part of the services transition life cycle. In this process, ITIL defines SKMS (Service Knowledge Management System) as "a set of information and data bases used to manage knowledge and information". The main role of this process, according to the ITIL library, is to improve the quality of decision-making.

At first analysis, there seems to be conflicting objectives. Why not use only ITIL and its knowledge management process?

The knowledge management concept of ITIL is a little confused. At a certain point of the definition, it is described that SKMS can be formed by CMDB (Configuration Management Database), repository of CIs and services and by CMS (a fuller repository of assets, information, known errors, etc.). The ITIL literature also mentions that SKMS can also contain information about coworker qualification, organizational data, supplier information, etc. It only states that "it can contain". At no moment does ITIL seek to determine how to obtain, structure, share or transmit knowledge, as it is only a general guide, and not a methodology.

Certain concepts of ITIL can be rather open to interpretation. My objective here is not to defend or criticize this, much to the contrary, I am only trying to interpret certain concepts to aid in elucidating a rather common question.

For me, at least, it is clear that the knowledge management process, of ITIL, is important and complete, has its objective well defined and without any doubt is fundamental within its proposal.

However, at no moment is it capable of aiding in knowledge management in the same manner as KCS does, focusing upon documentation of knowledge in the form of articles and related directly to supporting our help desk and customer care process.

Having said this, the notion that KCS is complementary to ITIL is confirmed even further.

How?

We can easily list certain examples where the use of articles of knowledge can be useful to ITIL. The following listing is not final, only representing certain examples of the complementation of KCS related to ITIL processes.

Table 2.2. Examples of use of articles of KCS knowledge in ITIL processes

ITIL process	Example of application of KCS article
Incident management and request fulfillment	Indeed, this is the central point of KCS: creation and maintenance of articles of knowledge related to incidents and requests. In this case, the association is self-explanatory.
Event management	Articles can be used for documentation of actions to be taken in response to events, for example. These articles can be created and maintained at other support levels (N2, N3) than at the level of operational staff who must respond to the events.

Problem management	The problems are a group of recurring incidents with similar symptoms or causes. In certain cases, it may be difficult to analyze them due to deficiency in their records. The articles related to these incidents can aid with important information, mainly that linked to the incidents; in many cases the practices of KCS, when mature, aid in nderstanding attributes related to the incidents and complement the documentation.
Access management	Articles can be used to document policies, rules and procedures related to permissions or non-permissions, or also security rules.
Change management	Important complementary documentation can be related to the environment, systems, etc. As with the problems, articles linked to incidents can aid in understanding scenarios and environments and configurations.
Release and deployment management	Articles can contain test plans, for example, as well as documentation linked to incidents caused by previous unsuccessful releases.

2.7. KCS process

The central element of the KCS process is knowledge, which must be appropriate, findable and reusable by the audience for which it is intended. It is cyclic, i.e., it is defined to be systematic and continuous.

All knowledge, the methods and results are based upon creating and updating articles. The articles represent contents, and the content is the most important element of a KCS process. According to the literal citation of the practices guide, **"the content is king"**.

For KCS, the content is king.

Knowledge, to become relevant and findable, is obtained and structured during the procedure of addressing issues or solving problems, in the context of the target audience. The study of content, in itself, generates knowledge. This is perhaps the central element of all KCS, which differentiates it from the traditional approaches to knowledge management.

According to data studied with members of the consortium, only 20% of the documented knowledge is used to solve 80% of issues. Thus, there is a high cost to maintain updated documentation which is rarely or never used.

Although the practices guide does not make any formal reference to the acronym PDCA or the Deming circle, the complete cycle of the KCS process finishes up representing exactly the parts of PDCA.

Conceptually, the process is divided into three components:

- Articles.
- Solve loop.
- Evolve loop.

KCS methodology uses a double loop process that complement each other. The **solve loop** is operational, while the **evolve loop** is driven to continuous improvement based on the analysis of the solve Loop experiences

Structurally, each loop is divided into practices, which in turn have techniques. As stated, the solve loop is related to the responder and the operational part of the process, while the evolve loop is related to the organization, control, monitoring and continuous improvement of the process.

Next, I will talk about the practices and techniques of each loop, seeking to summarize and indicate the most important concepts for understanding KCS. I recall once more that the intention is not to transcribe all the methodology, but to present a summary, in the most didactic manner possible, which allows understanding.

All this to be the basis for developing the practical roadmap which will be presented in the second part of this book.

Each loop is divided into practices, which in turn have techniques.

2.8. Articles

The articles represent the central element upon which KCS is based. According to the definition of the glossary, articles represent the collective experience – and, therefore, collaborative – of the organization which provides support to solving problems and answering questions. The articles must obtain the context of the requestor in his/her own words, as well as the perspective of the responder while resolving a problem or answering a question. Once obtained, the articles must be updated based upon demand and use, in the concept of "reusing is reviewing". This represents the maintenance life cycle of knowledge, which is continuous to the extent that knowledge evolves.

The articles can be used to store different types of content, including simple or complex questions, answers, procedures, instructions, etc.

In their basic structure, the articles must contain three perspectives:

- Perspective of the customer or end user. It includes their experience or perception of what is happening, as well as information about the environment which is relevant to the requirement. The description of a documented content must be the user's view of what is happening and the words thereof must be obtained in the context.

- Perspective of the responder. It is obtained during the resolution or response to a request, including cause, if applicable.

- Perspective of the organization. It is formed of data and information which support the control and management, such as situation of the article, date of creation and update, author, etc.

Articles must contain the perspectives of the customer, the responder and the organization.

We can summarize the articles as follows:

- They are the central element upon which KCS is based.
- They result from collective experience (collaborative, therefore).
- They must obtain the requestor's requirement in his/her own words.
- They must obtain the responder's perspective.
- They are updated based upon demand and use – "reusing is reviewing".

Reusing is reviewing.

2.9. Solve loop

A set of practices which represent a flow oriented towards solving problems or attending to users and customers. It is equivalent to the operational part of execution, with capture, update and publication of the articles, and, therefore, of knowledge.

2.9.1. Practice 1 – Capture

It concerns obtaining knowledge when issues are being resolved, in the context of the requestor, in his/her words, and of the responder's knowledge. To the extent that the tacit knowledge becomes explicit in the context of use, it becomes part of the article.

The practice of capture, or obtaining knowledge, is divided into four techniques:

Technique 1: capture of knowledge at the moment that it becomes explicit

As we mentioned previously, this is an innovating concept, perhaps the main one of the philosophy behind KCS. The methodology asserts that the traditional process of creating content unlinked from the moment when in touch with the requestor causes loss of important information for the documentation of the solution, besides usually being done by specialists in areas of knowledge who often use a language and a context which are not aligned with the user's reality.

An important principle of the methodology which deserves emphasis states that context is as important as content, and that it can be obtained better when in contact with the requestor.

Context is as important as content.

Technique 2: capture of knowledge in the user's context

As the knowledge is obtained when in contact with the requestor, it is natural and extremely desirable that this context is obtained, with the words and point of view thereof. We have already seen that the context is as important as the content. Now, it would not be a technical writer or a specialist, creating articles afterwards, that would be able to understand and acquire the user's context.

This is only possible if it is done during the contact. According to the methodology, this aids in localizing the knowledge, as other users can experience the same situations in the same context. Furthermore, the user's idiosyncrasy can probably be compatible with other users.

Oddly enough, according to the practices guide, an experiment made proves this idea. A doctor and a mechanic were requested to describe their diagnostic procedures of their respective work, documenting them. The practical observation, later, of their activities, showed that they acted differently from what they themselves had written. This, theoretically, means that they themselves lost information by lack of context related to their own procedures.

Technique 3: capture of relevant contents

This technique is important because it aids in an important definition, related to filtering the user's context. Although it is recommended to obtain the context, this does not mean literally seize what the user says. It is a subjective technique, which depends upon interpretation and common sense. The capacity of synthesis is an extremely valuable skill in people, and clearly not everybody has it to the same level. A clearer example applicable here would be in the case of requests created by email; in practice, many agents usually copy entire email contents and paste them in describing incidents, or, in this case, they could copy them in the contents of articles for documentation. Now, a whole email has a lot of information which is not relevant, and not unusually it takes a long time to extract what is relevant. In the second part, in the practical guide, we present a suggestion and examples of how to deal with this issue.

Technique 4: search arguments become part of the content

This practice complements the others, to the extent in which it is considered that the search arguments are part of the user's context, which can be used to improve articles or to guide the creation of new ones. This point is rather relevant to KCS: always seek to store the searches made, once search terms may become suitable knowledge.

As stated in practices guide, **"every search matters"**.

2.9.2. Practice 2 – Structuring

It is related to structuring the knowledge in a way which is consistent, following models and with a style which ensures clarity and understanding of the articles.

Technique 1: use of simple models

As the articles must have an appropriate structure of documented information, practice recommends using models which indicate which information attributes must be obtained. As different types of article can be defined, these models can equally be related to article types.

According to recommendation of the guide, the following attributes can be used to aid in context, consistency and facility of reading:

- Description: issue, symptom, question or problem.
- Environment: environment or configuration relevant to description.
- Solution: solution (final or surrounding) applied to the issue, question or problem. The solution usually corresponds to the answer to a request or a workaround for a problem.
- Cause: if applicable.
- Metadata: control data of the article, as who updated it, when, situation, etc.

Technique 2: complete thoughts instead of complete sentences

Rather aligned with technique 3 of the previous practice, this technique again reinforces the importance of synthesis and clarity of what is obtained.

2.9.3. Practice 3 – Reuse

One of the main elements of this practice concerns elimination of rework, by using the knowledge base when looking for a resolution to an issue; maybe that same issue has already been resolved and time is saved.

Searching the knowledge base should become a standard activity for agents. The expression used in the guide is "search early, search often".

Technique 1: search early, search often

This technique practically represents a mantra of KCS. Before starting the request resolution process, search the knowledge base. Even before creating a new article, search again to make sure that you are not creating a redundant article.

Search early, search often – a mantra of KCS.

Technique 2: understanding of collective knowledge

The principle behind this technique basically lies in avoiding rework.

It is using some knowledge already existing, preferably documented in the form of an article, to speed up diagnosis being executed.

Technique 3: linking

One part of this technique is related to linking articles to others. As a golden rule, the practice recommends that articles are succinct and summarized, trying if possible to maintain them on one or a few pages. When a great quantity of content is required, it is advisable to segment it into several articles and link them.

The other part concerns relating articles to the issue or problem, more precisely to indicate which article or articles were used in the solution.

This linking is an extremely important element because it represents the efficacy of the articles, considering that an article which is used to resolve an issue is something extremely desirable. One of the main indicators of KCS concerns exactly this: the percentage of issues resolved with the aid of articles, which is measured by the very existence of this type of link.

2.9.4. Practice 4 – Improvement

The central element in this practice is "reusing is reviewing". The attendants must become responsible for the contents with which they interact. If an attendant finds a content which (s)he does not understand, or wrong, (s)he must correct it or mark it for someone to correct. The expression in the guide for this is flag it or fix it.

Agents must become responsible for the contents with which they interact.

Technique 1: reusing is reviewing

The concept is simple, but extremely smart. Every time that an attendant has contact with an article, there is a potential occasion for reviewing. Whether obtaining a new context or new configuration of the user, or perceiving by his/her knowledge and experience that the contents can be improved and updated.

Technique 2: flag it or fix it

As a complement of the previous technique, upon reusing the information, the latter can and must be reviewed. Reviewing, in this case, means that the attendant can update the information, or if (s)he is not technically qualified or does not have time to update it at that moment, (s)he can mark it as outstanding to be updated.

Technique 3: update permissions

This item is related to a type of qualification certificate which is granted to people to execute functions in the process of updating information, in accordance with what the methodology calls authorization levels. Further details about permissions are looked at in the practice content health of the evolve loop.

2.10. Evolve loop

They are practices which form a continuous evaluation and evolution system which integrates organizational processes and people. This component is equivalent to the control and management part.

2.10.5. Practice 5 – Content health

This practice essentially concerns checking the quality of the knowledge base. On one hand, the features of collaborative, just-in-time update and collective property, in real time, all those presented in the solve loop, bring the benefit of agility, acquiring context, etc.

On the other hand, this leads to a very great dependence upon the competence and individual capacity of the people who collaborate in group, which can entail a very great variation in the standard of the results. Aware of this, the methodology foresees practices which allow constantly planning and reviewing the quality of the contents created.

Technique 1: article structure

This technique concerns the definition of the structure of articles, in terms of organization and consistency of the information. A structure for the articles must be defined so that, when dealing with an issue (solve loop), the responders provide the relevant information in appropriate manner, and thereby facilitating its later localization (and understanding). A well-defined structure is a fundamental element for obtaining knowledge value.

An appropriate structure ensures that the articles of the knowledge base are findable and usable by the audience for which they are intended.

The recommendation of KCS is that the articles have the following minimum structure:

- Description of the issue, problem or question.
- Environment.
- Resolution.
- Cause (if applicable).
- Metadata.

These elements were already in Practice 2, Technique 1. In spite of the redundancy, it is worth pointing out that the focus there is the issue or problem solving itself, whereas here we deal with the planning of the structure which must be filled during the issue or problem solving.

It also needs to be made clear that these attributes suggested do not necessarily exhaust the subject of the structure. Different types of article can have different structure requirements.

Technique 2: article lifecycle

The methodology defines, in this technique, the recommended flow that an article must follow between creation, review and publication. Different statuses are defined in which the articles are according to their life cycle, as well as the possible transitions between them.

The possible statuses of an article, according to KCS, are listed below.

- Work in progress (WIP): articles which contain all the information of context and environment, but do not yet have a documented solution, requiring a finishing.
- Draft: the article already has a solution, but as yet there is no certainty about its reliability due to lack of confirmation.
- Approved: article complete and considered to be ready to be used.
- Published: the article is approved and released to be used outside the organization, typically by customers or end users.
- Technical review: status in which an article is published and can be being used, but, due to the complexity of the subject, a technical review is desirable, to be executed by specialists in the subject. This status is considered to be optional by the methodology.
- Compliance review: similar to the previous status, except that the review required is for adaption to a policy, standard or procedure of the organization. This status is also considered to be optional by the methodology.
- Rework: status assigned to an article which is not compatible with the structure standard and must be reviewed. This status is also considered to be optional by the methodology.
- Archive: generally applicable to articles which have no more value.

As a general rule, to the extent that the articles improve through reuse and ensuing review, they can be made available for a larger audience, until they are made available for the external public. A concept used for this is called "visibility matrix", with which the permissions of viewing and access of the articles are defined.

An interesting observation of the practices guide concerning the statuses of the articles mentions an expression referred to as "stagnation of KCS". According to this concept, the presence of different statuses of the articles can indicate that they are undergoing reviews and updates. Not that the articles must constantly change status, but this is a sign that they are being reviewed and updated.

The existence of articles in different statuses can indicate that the system is operational, with the articles being reviewed and updated.

Technique 3: standard development of contents

This technique refers to the creation of standards of content to be used during the creation of articles. As the name indicates, it is at this moment that the standards, criteria and rules under which the articles will be created are defined. The result is the creation of a document similar to a standard or procedure.

A question which may have arisen is: what exactly is the difference between the structure (Technique 1 of this practice) and the standard of contents, mentioned here?

The structure of contents is concerned with defining which attributes, or which types of information, must be registered. While the standard refers to the way of documenting.

It is related to the language and style of writing.

Certain elements recommended, which can be created to aid in defining standard of contents, are as follows:

- Quick reference guide.
- Definition of structure of articles (as defined in Technique 1 of this practice).
- Examples of good and bad articles.
- Models.
- Style guides.

Technique 4: article quality management

This technique is vitally important for the system, as, through several methods, it checks the quality of the articles and consequently of the system as a whole.

There are five elements which contribute to the quality of the articles of KCS:

1) AQI – Articles Quality Index

It concerns a KPI which considers measurements of attributes important and relevant to the quality of the articles, forming a metric which allows the evaluation and view of the evolution of the contribution of people and groups with the passage of time. The attributes of which the evaluation is recommended by KCS for forming AQI are:

- Duplication of articles.
- Evaluation if the articles are complete in their structure proposed, involving description, environment, cause, etc. – in accordance with the structure defined (Practice 5, Technique 1).
- Clarity of contents, following the line of "complete thoughts and not complete sentences".
- Consistent relationship of the title with the contents.
- Correction of the hyperlinks, if there are any.
- Correction of the metadata.

The concept, as in any KPI, consists of defining evaluation values for each attribute and then weighting them, to at the end generate a numerical result – in this case, AQI. This measurement can be made by the article author and by a group of people.

It is clear in the practices guide, as if it could be otherwise, that each organization can and must seek measurements and metrics which are most appropriate to its reality.

2) **Permissions schema**, mentioned previously, especially with the concept of a coaching (mentoring) function, so that the people with suitable qualification aid the others in maintaining the quality of the articles.

3) **Standardization of contents**, in accordance with the structure defined in Practice

5, Technique 1.

4) **Performance evaluation model**, to be detailed further in Practice 7.

5) **Concept of flag it or fix it**, theoretically representing a systematic and continuous

operation to improve quality – Practice 4, Technique 2.

Technique 5: creation of articles in evolve loop

So far, we have repeatedly seen that KCS stipulates the creation and update of contents when dealing with issues or problems, in the just-in-time modality.

In this technique, however, there is also considered the possibility of creating contents before being in touch with requestors, i.e., proactive content creation. Although it seems to be an antithesis of everything which the KCS methodology advocates, there are acknowledged situations where the traditional model of creation prior to content must be followed.

Certain situations where this may be necessary are, for example, those where:

- The content to be generated depends upon specialists who are not in the front line, as level 2 and 3 analysts.

- The content type is related to procedures, instructions and standards – a practical example of this is the article structure guide, for example, which must exist before the system begins to be used.
- The content must be generated and made available proactively to end users, on the Web, as roadmaps, guides or guidelines concerning products or services.

Technique 6: New x known analysis

This technique corresponds to a good example of the evaluation of continuous improvement of KCS. It represents one of the most important points of the methodology, in dealing with the objective of the system and measurement of quality.

To the extent that knowledge is created and updated, the number of incidents or requisitions which have a documented solution tends to increase – with the repeated reuse of knowledge. It all makes sense, as theoretically the system is cyclical, systematic and continuous. In theory, with increased use, more and more solutions which represent user problems and requirements are documented.

This technique is directly related to this concept. When an issue is resolved and a solution exists in the form of an article in the knowledge base, the technique recommends that this link is indicated; this situation corresponds to the term '**KNOWN**' for KCS, referring to *known documentation* – this linking, at an operational level, was explained in Practice 3, Technique 3.

In cases when a new article is created during issue resolution, a new link is created, being considered '**NEW**', according to the terminology.

One of the main objectives of this technique is to monitor, over time, the percentage of issues resolved with a link to an article created previously.

In this same analysis, other indicators are evaluated, as, for example, the quality and consistency of the existing link, and if perchance there may have been issues resolved without a link recorded, even if there exists a corresponding article in the knowledge base.

This technique is composed of four steps:

- Scope definition. Definition of type or categorization of issues which will be evaluated, as well as a period. The scope is fundamental because, in practice, it is not feasible to analyze all the occurrences.
- Data collection. It corresponds to collecting data as per the scope defined.
- Incident analysis. Analysis of the incidents and other indicators.
- Identification and discussion of opportunities. Identification of trends, indication of causes and possible definition of action plan for adjustments.

KCS presents a spreadsheet of evaluation model known x new with the attributes to be evaluated which can be downloaded from the consortium site. In the second part of the of the book we shall present a practical evaluation proposition.

Technique 7: Success in self-help

According to KCS, self-help is every type of interaction where the end user or customer achieves a solution for his/her problem without interaction with any attendant.

The success of self-help depends upon a good level of maturity of the system, as the definition of the contents most appropriate to the users and their format can be a task which takes time. There is also a cultural factor which needs to be evaluated, in the sense of encouraging users to try to seek their solutions for themselves.

In the description of this technique, KCS suggests four key criteria which can be indicators of success in self-help by users:

- Volume and speed of generation of articles for end users.
- Facility of localization of content by users.
- Navigation of users in the portal, which must be a simple and intuitive experience.
- Marketing, in the sense of disclosure and sensitization to drive the use of self-help resources. The following comment described in the practices guide is of relevant interest: one cannot expect a model of the type "it suffices to make available for them to come" to function.

Important remark

The result of a survey made among the participants of the consortium indicates that the benchmark is that the users or customers must find what they seek between 40% and 50% of the time.

Technique 8: Evaluation of the value of articles

To the extent that KCS is consolidated, the knowledge base tends to grow. It is desirable to evaluate the value of the articles in this base, and not only record their quantity.

The value of the articles can be evaluated from three perspectives:

- Reuse frequency. The most usual way of measuring reuse is related to the use of the article to resolve requirements, i.e., the same linking concept presented in technique 6 (known x new). There are no restrictions, however, to using as criterion the number of displays, or also the number of positive evaluations, for example.
- Value of the set of articles. This indicator, according to the guide, is more related to the success in self-help, as it indicates that the interventions or calls to the support area cease to be executed by the requestors.
- Reference frequency. Very little is said about this metric, indeed only a paragraph. It would be something related to an article which uses the reference of others for a solution. The guide itself states that the

measurement of this is rather complex and difficult, not being looked at.

2.10.6. Practice 6 – Process integration

This practice is related to two approaches.

One of them is related to the integration of the help desk or customer care software, such as incidents and requisitions, with the knowledge base control software. It is explained extensively how important it is that this integration is transparent, so that the operation is made feasible as if it were in a single operating environment.

Clearly, this subject is related to cases where different software is used for each one of the purposes.

The second approach of this technique is directed to the guidance of problem solving practices, or a structured problem solution process.

Technique 1 – Structured problem solution

In this technique, a whole topic is dedicated to the contextualization of structured problem solution, with theoretical concepts and examples.

As a reference to the content which is proposed, two books are mentioned, one called "The Rational Manager", of Charles Kepner and Benjamin Tregoe (www.kepner-tregoe.com/tools/books/the-new-rational-manager/), and "The

7 habits of highly effective people", of Stephen R. Covey (www.stephencovey.com/7habits/7habits.php).

Oddly enough, the analogy presented in the guide is related to the importance of preserving the scene of a crime, capturing all the details, to only then move on to the investigation phase.

The structured problem solution process consists of two simple and important concepts:

- Search to understand before searching to resolve. This means understanding the context of the customer and preserving it – in this case, capturing it (documenting it).
- Search early, search often. Often the search can lead to one or more articles which describe similar situations.

The fundamental concept behind all the idea is to search a lot before starting the diagnosis. Even though a result found is not the ideal or final solution, it can present information which aids in the solution which is being sought.

If no article is found, it goes on to the analysis phase, which could also be understood as being investigation, when new information and clarification need to be studied.

One care which must be taken, which is emphasized in the guide, is to avoid going on very quickly to the diagnosis (investigation) phase, with the risk of reaching hasty conclusions before listening to the customer or being certain that articles with the information required were not located.

It is highly advisable to take care to not go directly to the diagnostic phase before capturing the customer's context and carefully searching the knowledge base.

Technique 2 – Transparent technology integration (software)

It is directly related to tool integration, including software of incident and requisitions with knowledge base software and Web portals. This integration must be as simplified as possible, so that both, incidents and articles, are easily viewed and updated in a single interface.

Examples of workflows and interfaces – with the consideration that there is not one interface which is suitable for all –are presented in this technique.

According to the recommendation of the practices guide, an ideal flow of integrated knowledge base and help desk tools must include the following functions:

- Search in the knowledge base using information of the incident as the basis to start or refine the search.
- Link of articles and incidents.
- Viewing of article linked to incident, in both directions.
- Possibility of modification of articles during the reuse.
- Creation of articles from incident information.
- Collaborating with the specialists of areas for solutions (the guide explicitly mentions chat or email, but obviously other means can be used).

Technique 3 – Search technology for KCS

This technique defends the requirement of investment in technology which handles more effective search for content, including, if necessary, mechanisms of indexation, which deal with smart search. Obviously, the search for contents is fundamental, as organization and capture are of no use if they are not accessed.

The importance of the relevance in the search results is also described. The relevance is related to the context of that which the user is searching, a smart search system having to 'understand' what is most relevant to the user and present the results as priorities.

The difference in the nature of computer and human languages is also commented upon, and how this can affect the searching. Although it is not mentioned explicitly, the assumptions described in this technique are very much aligned with certain areas of artificial intelligence, as NLU - Natural Language Understanding, for example, which is no more than making computers understand human language and transform this understanding into understanding of intentions.

Another factor emphasized is the importance of indexing contents of different sources to be searched in a centralized way. In other words, this means that a knowledge base is not necessarily a single database, but is formed of different bases which are searched as if they were a single repository.

Technique 4 – Closed loop feedback for all the system

My interpretation of the concept is that this technique represents a continuous feedback cycle, as KCS creates a learning system based upon the experience obtained through contacts with users and customers. Then, it involves the evaluation of the content created and its use to improve the system as a whole and also to aid in improving the services and products delivered to the users or customers, thereby closing the circuit (or cycle).

The practices guide draws an analogy with the health area, which has moved its efforts to prevention, instead of only being concerned with healing. Likewise, service companies have sought to act in causes of problems, aiming to reduce them or eliminate them, avoiding reactive incidents or problems.

Regarding KCS itself, the technique recommends establishing the root cause with corrective actions to eliminate the problem.

Author's note

That which is described in this technique refers to the practices of problem management, of ITIL.

2.10.7. Practice 7 – Performance evaluation

One of the practices must not be elected as being the most important, at the risk of giving the impression that the others are less relevant, but, without the shadow of a doubt, if it were done, this would be one of the candidates.

It concerns evaluating the efficacy of the system as a whole, even being called performance evaluation.

That is why the following elements are covered:

- Attributions (functions or responsibilities) and model of people's permissions (licenses).
- Adoption phases (akin to maturity levels) and the requirements for each one of them.
- Evaluation of who is creating value, through triangulation – based upon the concepts of balanced scorecard, of Kaplan and Norton.
- A scenario which shows the value of certain measurements.
- A list of measurements, their definitions and uses.

Technique 1 – Attributions and model of permissions (licensing)

The concept of permission, or license, is presented as a metaphor for the permission to drive automobiles, which starts with theoretical training, going on to obtaining a provisional permission, then a full one and, in accordance with the experience and skill, permission to drive vehicles of greater complexity.

The first learning is in a classroom, but only practice internalizes behavior and competences until they become natural.

The adoption of KCS is like learning to drive automobiles. The first learning is in a classroom, but only practice internalizes behavior and competences until they become natural.

Probably the greatest barrier to adopting the methodology is the change of culture of the organization, to understand and accept the concept of collaboration and socialization of knowledge.

To do so, certain functional responsibilities necessary to the process are identified. They are as follows:

- Leaders. The managers must be the leaders. They must define the vision of success at the level at which they perform and support the content developers, deciding how the work must be done and defining standards.

- Content developers:
    o Candidate. Basic user of knowledge base, familiar with initial techniques of search and capture and with basic knowledge of KCS.
    o Contributor. (S)he creates, modifies and reviews articles for a certain audience, usually formed of the internal public.
    o Publisher. All the attributions of the contributor and the qualification to publish for the external public.
    o Mentor. Agent of change, specialist in KCS, supports the development of competences and proficiency in KCS.
    o Specialist in the domain of knowledge. Deep knowledge of technical subjects of a certain area.

It is also advisable that a KCS board is established, which meets periodically to discuss issues related to the system and possible improvements.

The guide explains in detail the attributions and responsibilities suggested for each function and also deals with establishing a people evaluation and evolution system in a kind of career plan, through attributions.

Technique 2 – Phases of adoption

The participants of the consortium defined as another mantra that KCS is not a destination, but a journey, as it consists of a process of learning and continuous improvement. It makes sense, therefore, that the journey has intermediary milestones and goals, thereby evaluating its evolution.

In this technique the phases are described, together with the benefits, measurements and conditions of evolution (change of phase). According to KCS, the understanding of each phase is critical, as the level and type of benefits which can be expected vary. It is mentioned explicitly that KCS can stagnate if the focus of management and measurements do not change to the extent that the phase changes. Another risk can lie in establishing goals or expectations which are not compatible with the level of maturity of the organization.

KCS can stagnate if the focus of management and measurements do not change to the extent that the phase changes.

The four phases of adoption are as follows:

- Planning and design.
- Adoption.

- Proficiency.
- Leverage of the knowledge base.

The following table presents the focus suggested for each phase, as well as the organizational measures suggested as an evaluation reference for advancing in the phases. It is model coherent with the so-called maturity levels.

Table 2.3. Phases of adoption of KCS, management focus and organizational measurements

Phase	Management focus	Sample of organizational measures
1. Planning and design	- Definition of tools to be used - Collection of baseline measures - Determination of internal and external realistic expectations	- Top management support - Project deliveries draft
2. Adoption	- Creation of internal understanding and sensitization through initial competence - Internal reference	- Known x new proportion of incidents - Link rate - Article quality index

3. Proficiency	- Creation and maturity of knowledge base -Increased process efficiency - Reduced time for proficiency (qualification of new coworkers for the work) - Improved people collaboration and satisfaction	- Cost by incident - Solution capacity - Solution percentage in first contact - Time for enabling new coworkers and new technologies - Time for publishing articles
4. Knowledge base leverage	- Resource use optimization - Reduced support costs - Increased customer success and employee satisfaction -Improved products and services	- Support percentage cost - Customer satisfaction and loyalty - Coworker satisfaction, turnover - Successful customer self-service use

It is recommended that the organization makes a careful evaluation to check its condition of positioning and change of phase.

A critical point is to take care not to establish objectives or expectations not compatible with the maturity level of the organization.

Technique 3 – Balanced scorecard

With the understanding of the attributions, or functions, which the people perform we can move on to defining metrics and goals for the team. The recommendation of KCS is to use the balanced scorecard, of Norton and Kaplan, for the following factors:

- Link of individual goals and objectives to those of the group.
- Viewing of performance from multiple points of view, the so-called perspectives.
- Distinction between process indicators and business indicators.

Note

If anyone wants to remind themselves of or know more deeply the concepts of the balanced scorecard, I recommend the book "Kaplan and Norton in Practice" (2004).

One of the elements highlighted in this technique is the differentiation between process and business indicators. The former measures the result of the execution of the processes, generally being related to the activities, while the latter deal with the efficacy of the processes for business. In the second part of the book I shall detail this distinction further, with some practical examples.

The KCS glossary uses a known terminology in the performance evaluation management systems, defined as follows:

- **Leading indicators**: they are quantifiable activities, which must be measured to identify trends. They are equivalent to the KM process indicators.
- **Lagging indicators**: they are qualitative indicators, related to the results. They correspond to the business indicators.

If there is excessive focus upon the indicators of the process related to the creation of knowledge, with quantitative goals for creating articles, for example, certain to say the least undesirable results can be obtained, as, for example:

- Unexpected qualitative results, as people can create contents without criteria, only aiming at quantity.
- Deviation from the main objective, leaving quality aside.
- Control of indicators without value for business.

Another fundamental element in the system performance evaluation is the integration of three different measurement perspectives:

- Process indicator trends.
- Article quality index.
- Business indicators, with their goals.

These three perspectives are called "triangulation".

Triangulation represents measuring value creation, which cannot be counted directly.

According to the metaphor of the KCS practices guide itself, triangulation is a concept analogous to that of the systems of GPS (Global Positioning System), which establish the positioning based upon the triangulation of data obtained from several satellites.

It is important to bear in mind that each organization must seek to adapt metrics relevant to its own reality.

2.10.8. Practice 8 – Leadership and communication

The adoption of KCS leads to transformation in organizations, and this requires strong leadership. Understanding the relevance of KCS is of paramount importance for success.

It is extremely necessary that the deployment of KCS is aligned with the strategic objectives of the organization. Obviously, everything seen so far herein depends upon people, both at the leadership level and concerning the people involved at the tactical and operational levels.

The leaders must create a healthy culture which encourages individual commitment and participation of people, through an effective communication plan, clear definitionof functions and a system which recognizes the efforts and results. It is not productive to have leadership capacity without a good communication plan.

The guide describes practices which aid the leaders to:

- Define organizational metrics and goals for business objectives.
- Capitalize on the motivation factors for adopting KCS.
- Encourage people in the collaborative environment.
- Obtain executive support for the KCS initiative.
- Communicate with each other.

Efficient leadership is the fundamental requirement for the success of KCS.

Technique 1 – Alignment with an objective with commitment

There is a greater likelihood of people taking part in a knowledge management practice if they believe in the objectives of the organization. Furthermore, anther motivating factor is the feeling of execution and acknowledgement.

It is essential, therefore, that people know the objectives of the company and understand where they are inserted in the organization. Often it can seem that the service executed by a support analyst is far from these objectives, which is not true. It is a great challenge, therefore, the transformation which is required so that people understand their importance to the company.

Technique 2 – Creation of a strategic model

It concerns a simple, but powerful, document, which links the benefits of KCS to the goals of the organization, forming the basis of the communication plan and the basis for obtaining the support of top management.

This strategic model aligns objectives of the stakeholders which are fundamental:

- Organization.
- Coworkers.
- Customers.
- Business partners, if applicable.

Basically, what the technique proposes is to define, for each stakeholder:

- Business objective (what).
- Approach (how).
- Contribution which KCS can bring to business.

An example mentioned to aid in developing the model is customer loyalty as being one of the main organizational goals. For such, the average solution time of incidents is important, and, therefore, it is a metric which must be considered.

The content of this technique spreads into other concepts and examples which can be taken into account in preparing the strategic model.

The issue of ROI (return on investment) is also looked at in this technique.

Technique 3 – Furtherance of group work

Seeing that collaboration is a fundamental pillar of KCS, this technique is concerned with the organizational and cultural aspects of group work. The creation of a culture of collaboration and the acceptance of the concept of collective ownership of are the leader's responsibility.

The methodology is based upon the concepts of Patrick Lencioni's book, "The Five Dysfunctions of a Team" (www.tablegroup.com/books/dysfunctions), to analyze the possible dysfunctions present in groups and the ways of reducing them.

Technique 4 – Attention to internal motivational factors

It stresses the importance of maintaining people motivated, so that the focus on collaboration is maintained. Two literary references are mentioned, one of them being an article of the Harvard Business Review, which is one of the reprints most required of all times, called "One more time, How do you motivate employees", of Frederick Herzberg (http://synchronit.com/downloads/freebooks/herzberg.pdf).

The other reference is the book "Drive", of Daniel Pink (www.danpink.com/books/drive/), mandatory reading for all KCS managers.

Technique 5 – Incentive and acknowledgement programs

According to this technique, to motivate people and further the adoption of KCS many organizations adopt reward practices. In accordance with the practices guide, this type of program is not easy to be adopted, and is often confused regarding the real objectives, motivating only quantitative production, not focusing upon quality.

The participants of the consortium place in this technique part of their lessons learnt and state that acknowledgement is a secondary effect of doing things in the right way.

Some of the principles of this type of program, for it to be successful, are:

- Use of legitimate metrics.
- Alignment with the organizational objectives.
- Clear definition of the start and end of the incentive programs.
- Integration with people's activities.
- Balance between personal and group rewards.
- Equal opportunities of taking part.

Technique 6 – Communication is the key

The main subject dealt with in this technique is no novelty in the business world.

Effective communication is a tremendous challenge. According to the guide, a message must attain its audience 36 times before being absorbed and understood. Then, certain other facts are presented corroborating the idea that entrepreneurial communication is one of the main factors people complain about.

The challenge proposed in this technique is to assemble an efficacious communication plan concerning KCS, which is in fact a marketing plan, called endomarketing.

The recommendations for a good plan are as follows:

- Definition of target audience.
- Definition of the main message.
- Leaving clear the personal benefits and not only the organizational ones.
- Publishing frequently asked questions about KCS.
- Dealing with objections.
- Using the concept of elevator pitch to sell the idea of KCS in a brief manner – traditionally thirty seconds, as per the concept.
- Using appropriate means of communication.

2.11. Conclusion of the first part

We have reached the end of the first part of the book, where I have sought to present conceptual definitions of knowledge management and the KCS methodology as the foundation for the second part, where a guide will be proposed for the planning and implementation of a system based upon KCS practices, but adapted to a reality which makes it feasible for companies of any size.

Second Part

Planning and Implementation of Knowledge Management and KCS in IT Services

3. Contextualization of Assistance in IT Services

Although the amplitude of IT services is extensive, the focus of this book is related to assistance to internal users or external customers, in technical support, customer care, shared services or ombudsmen.

Depending upon the role which each person exercises in an organization, his/her involvement can be more or less operational, or more or less managerial, and thus there can certainly be differing interpretations, objectives and views.

First and foremost, let us go to the areas themselves.

First, let us look at the technical support and service desk areas. Conceptually, in accordance with the ITIL best practices library definition, the service desk renders IT technical support assistance services, with the responsibility of being the sole point of contact between the user and all the assistance process.

We are not going to enter into detail here regarding the ITIL library or service desk. For the purposes of all the concepts dealt with in this book, technical support and service desk are similar and, to simplify the language used, will be called support.

The main purpose of support is to aid its users or customers resolve their difficulties. Here an exception is made for a new comment concerning the ITIL library.

In accordance with it, support must re-establish the normal operating condition of users as quickly as possible, and these events of abnormality are called incidents. A problem is a set of similar incidents without cause resolved. Anyway, the common point is that a user or customer has a difficulty which prevents him/her from executing his/her work and requires the aid of support to return to working normally. This is one part of what support does; the other is to attend to requests, also known as requisitions. So, requisitions are requests to attend to a requirement, or service, which does not represent a failure or abnormal occurrence. To give an example: an unexpected failure in software which the user uses is an incident, but a new access to software which the user needs is a requisition.

And why exactly is this important?

Because the treatment given to one and the other will probably have to be different. Obligations of priority and time and agreements are different.

So far, we have established what the function of support is.

And as for shared services, What are they? What do they do?

Shared service centers are areas which are responsible for the execution and the handling of specific operational tasks, attending to users or customers from other areas of the organization.

They are established in the cases where companies have several units dispersed geographically with similar functions and areas. The shared services, as the name indicates, centralizes the assistance, or the area, or also the process and agents to it in a shared manner with several units distributed.

Usually the shared services execute assistance to requisitions, although there are cases in which they aid in solving incidents.

What do the support services or shared services have in common, indeed?

Both aim to attend to user and customer demands, no matter what their nature. There is a requirement by a user or customer and, and on the other an established process or area, with material and human resources, which aim to attend to this requirement. Again, of purposes of employing simplified language, we are going to treat any type of requirement, whether incident or requisition, as a demand.

Let us go ahead, now analyzing the processes of attending to demands, from the point of view of knowledge management.

Let us first assume certain premises:

- Different types of demand can be expected.
- Very simple to the most complex demands can arise.
- Each type of demand requires specific knowledge to be attended to.
- Depending upon the criticality of the demand (serious problem, for example, or urgent requirement), the term for the solution can be longer or shorter.
- Knowledge is required even for knowing what the user desires or needs.
- The knowledge required changes practically every day, as new products are launched, modified or updated. The users also discover forms of use.
- Knowledge is also required to know how to seek the solution, with a critical sense to filter which solutions

are applicable or viable (an exaggerated example would be a blind person trying to search in Google for a solution to resolve a problem of heating in a nuclear reactor and resolve the common problem of heating).

Taking these premises as a starting point, we can try to imagine what the perfect and utopian scenario would be, regarding assistance:

- Attendants with sufficient knowledge for all and any assistance.
- Even though each attendant were unable to master all the areas, the sum of the knowledge of all the attendants would cover all the areas of knowledge required.
- In this case, each demand would be sent to the attendant with knowledge in the respective area.
- The attendants of each area would always be able to transfer their knowledge to others to provide coverage in case of vacations or leaving the company, or also to new coworkers hired.
- Besides attending to the users, the attendants would manage to update themselves and absorb new knowledge required every day.

So, dear reader. Did you find it simple? Easy?

I can try to guess your answers. NO for the first question, probably NO for the second. The bad news is that you are only too right regarding the first one and are probably right regarding the second one.

It is to handle questions like these, from the premises and utopian imagination presented, that there is knowledge management, and the good news (there always has to be some, afterall) is that it can be applied to support.

Before anyone gets too excited, however, I can state that, unless you the reader perform a miracle, one cannot expect to resolve 100% of the solution for these items. What one can have is a better result than that obtained without applying the principles and techniques of knowledge management.

3.1. Knowledge management planning

Why implement knowledge management in the assistance area of my company?

Alignment with business, first and foremost

It seems too obvious, even a cliché. Any initiative in companies must be aligned with business. However, what exactly does this mean for the knowledge management initiative?

Even more as we are dealing with implementing knowledge management practices to attend to users, then it seems that this is very far from business itself. Perhaps, not so much.

First, we can be dealing with support in software or service companies, where this is practically the end activity of the company, or at least a fundamental part of the value chain.

The shared services areas exist and aim to attend to their users.

They were probably created to provide competitiveness to their organizations. Even the support in IT areas which are not the end activity plays a vital role, as it supports the delivery of value with the IT itself executes.

Anyway, when we speak about alignment of knowledge management with business, we can be referring to the highest level, strategic objectives of organizations, or intrinsic objectives of areas, which in turn collaborate with the fulfillment of greater objectives.

Let us begin with the beginning, pardoning redundancy. Above all, it is important to establish the objective, seek the reason for starting any knowledge management effort. This beginning may be simple, or not, but it can be related to the attempt to answer a single question:

Why implement knowledge management in the assistance area of my company?

It is important to note that the answer expected is not the definition, or part of the definition, of knowledge management itself. It is no use answering here something like "organizing, obtaining and transmitting knowledge" or "retaining knowledge". What must be sought is an answer which satisfies some business objective, or at least of the area.

It seems to be becoming complicated... some examples may perhaps help to elucidate it. It is worth mentioning that several answers can be relevant, which would generate several objectives.

Brainstorming – Why make an effort to implement knowledge management practices?

- Increase the number of demands resolved in the first assistance (considering as first assistance the first contact of the attendant with the demand, either by telephone speaking with the user or else obtaining the demand in a line of holdovers).
- Reduce the time of attending to demands (time elapsed between the recording of the demand by the user and the solution of the requirement).
- Improve the quality of the solutions presented (which could be considered to be, for example, reducing rework or redispatch of similar demands).
- Improve the perception which the customers have of the service rendered.
- Increase customer satisfaction and retention.
- Improve business profitability.

I take the liberty of inviting you to write your ideas.

All the previous answers are examples of objectives which can be defined and expected as a result of initiatives related to knowledge management. Each company can have its own, but probably many arrive at something very similar, due to the nature of the support services and their reason for being. Note that the items can represent objectives of different stakeholders.

If you want to go deeper in the formalization of these objectives, segment them in accordance with the stakeholder customers, attendants and company.

To facilitate, the approach of process and the identification of certain key elements can help.

3.2. Process approach

What we call here process approach is nothing more than beginning the work of planning from the support process, i.e., thinking about the process itself. We are not going to enter into detail about process management, as it concerns a very broad issue. Only for reference, we would be dealing with BPM (Business Process Management), so that we would also have a standardized manner of representing the design of the processes.

It is probable that many readers already know BPM, which is excellent, as it facilitates the understanding of what is suggested below.

In a generic and simplified form, we can state that a process is a set of activities executed to attain a determined end, having an input, an output (or a result produced) and rules which concern its functioning. A process must also have its performance measured, i.e., have indicators related to its performance. Even though in your company you do not have a process which is mapped out and formally defined, it is certain that the assistance executed in help desk or customer care has an input, activities are executed and a result is produced.

In the case of support, the input is almost invariably a demand arising from a user's requirement. The activities correspond to the actions executed for the assistance. Ideally, in the documentation of the process, such activities are detailed to a level which allows the exact understanding of the important actions which are executed and what is to be controlled. In fact, there is no rule to define what the ideal level of detail is. If a detail level which is too low is defined, the objective of the approach by process is lost. For example, the most generic level of definition which could be imagined for a support process would be composed of three mapped activities:

1. Receiving the request or general demand.

2. Executing the assistance.

3. Giving the solution to the user.

Let us take as an example activity 2, the execution of the assistance itself. Certainly, if we think about how things happen in daily operation, it shall be possible to identify a greater level of detail. One of the ways of discovering how to detail the activities is through questions. Certain questions which may be relevant to this study, for example, could be:

- Who receives the demands for the first user's contact?
- Is it a fixed person or a fixed group of people?
- Is a record made about the demand to be assisted to?
- If the first agent does not resolve the demand, how does it proceed? To whom is it forwarded?
- If this forwarding occurs, is it directly to a person or to a group?

With only a few questions ideas may arise of how to detail further the activities executed. On the other hand, excessive details will not contribute to the objective proposed, and will only make control and management more difficult. Merely to illustrate, let us imagine that an activity is something like "giving return to the user", related to maintaining the user aware about an event relevant to the assistance. In this specific example, it would be useless to decompose this activity into

"Open Outlook/Writer email/Send email". Clearly this example may appear absurd, but it was only used to reinforce a notion of the concept of greater or less details.

An important comment is appropriate here. During the mapping of your process, you may happen to see certain points which could be modified, improved, indeed – through the exercise of analytical thought you may arrive at a certain conclusion which leads to a modification or improvement in your process.

This would be excellent, as you were able to see opportunities for improvement. By way of curiosity and for knowledge, according to BPM, in this phase the process must be mapped as it is, and only later think about modifying it and optimizing it.

As we are not dealing with BPM in this book, it is only for informative purposes. What is important in our knowledge management context is, now, mapping the activities executed.

From the process presented in the previous figure, we have, therefore, the following activities mapped:

Table 3.1. Activities of the support process

Activity	Description
Start	First contact with the user, understanding the necessity and formally recording the request
Classification	Description, type and categorization, prioritization and other classifications applicable
Resolve @ Level 1	Resolution attempt @ level 1
Issue is resolved?	Decision
Yes - resolved	If the solution is satisfactory, record data referring to the solution
No – escalate level 2	Solution was not found, forwarding to second level
Resolve @ Level 2	Resolution attempt @ level 2
Record resolution	Record data referring to the solution
End	Close the request

Now that we have the activities of a process defined, let us go ahead. For each one of them, we are going to identify certain elements which will be important and will aid us for our sequence in knowledge management. These elements are described below.

3.3. Moments of truth

Particularly, I like this concept very much and consider it rather appropriate to apply in our objective. It was created by Jan Carlzon, when CEO of SAS Airlines, and is currently widely acknowledged in the business world. It is a concept used considerably in preparing strategic planning.

A moment of truth represents any occasion upon which the customer comes into contact with any aspect of the company and has some type of perception about it.

It corresponds to those occasions when the opinion can be strongly formed, albeit subjective. Often we ignore and do not pay attention to these moments, committing the mistake of focusing only on the process as if it were something hermetic and had nothing to do with the customers. Total misunderstanding.

Let us begin by a generic example, to then proceed to our support process. Let us think about our experience as customers in a restaurant.

Have you never had a similar situation in which, in spite of the food and the price, you feel that something is not right? It may be confusion in the waiting room, with a confused and disorganized queue, a feeling that others who arrived later went before you... and the heat? The waiting room is stuffy, it seems not to have air-conditioning.

Well, and then? When I sit down, I adore the food and am ready. Only the bill... ah, the bill... almost always comes wrong, charging things which I did not ask for. If it were not for the food and the price, I would never go back there.

Were you able to understand the context?

In this fictitious example, the end process is well done, the food is good and has a good price. Only there was a lack of concern with other aspects which are also important for customers, and these are defined as moments of truth. In the case of the restaurant, we could imagine that the moments of truth would be the following:

- Reception of the customers (reception and forwarding to tables. It is a moment which can really spoil one's mood, the perception related to the issue).
- Taking the order (attending to the customer after (s)he sits down, politely and attentively. It is no good sitting the customer at the table and leaving him/her waiting 45 minutes to take the order).
- Delivery of the order (considering that the customer chose a dish, the delivery in a reasonable time, or in the time indicated, is essential).
- Correct charging (charge for what was consumed).

Some people may be thinking that the moments of truth then and after all are all the activities, as that which is listed is everything which a restaurant does.

The answer is no. That which is listed is everything which a restaurant does and that the customer perceives directly, as was said in the definition of moments of truth.

A restaurant does many things backstage, as purchase of food, preservation, process of preparing, quality control, etc., etc. I imagine that now it is all clear, right?

Go back to your list of activities and identify which of them are moments of truth.

Return to thinking about your process, in your day-to-day, and check that there is no moment of truth which you did not list as an activity and then list it.

For the support process, some probable moments of truth are listed below. Make use of them to reflect about your process.

- Access: it concerns how the customer manages to arrive at support.
    - If it is by telephone, is the connection easy or is the line always busy?
    - Does it go through several levels of robotized responses, by IVR (interactive voice responses)? If it is by the switchboard operator, is the conversation polite and objective?
    - If the customer tries to make a request by portal, is access easily achieved? Does the system function? Was (s)he guided about how to use it?
- Assistance: executed by the agent.
    - Does (s)he hear what the customer want or need?
    - Is it friendly, considering if the customer is nervous? Does it deal well with this?
    - Does it give the impression that he is there to help?
- Efficacy: what the customer wants is to have his/her requirement resolved.
    - Does (s)he feel that calling support resolves the issue?
    - Does (s)he feel that when requesting something it will be handled?
- Information about rules of attending:

- When there is a requirement, as a problem, for example, is the customer informed about an estimated term for the solution, or at least for someone to call him/her back?
- If it is a service request, is it indicated when the service will be done by? If the assistance is franchised up to a certain limit or charged, is this left clear?

- Information about assistance:
  - After the initial contact, when so desiring, is the customer able to know about his/her request?
- Is it simple?
  - Or is it always the (in)famous "tell the whole story again"?

You can have others in your process, but regarding support it is not likely that the previous points do not represent moments of truth.

3.4. Critical points

Think about what can go wrong and that, if it does, will be bad.

Think about the problems which can occur in attending to your customers and, if they occur, what the probable or possible causes could be. These are your critical points.

Some examples of what can be critical in support assistance, to aid you in studying your reality:

- Certain wrong answers: wrong solution or guidance given by the agent to the user.

- o Depending upon who the user is or what (s)he requires, a wrong solution can be bad, terrible or catastrophic.
- Guidelines to update a system version done incorrectly can leave the user totally inoperative at a critical moment for the operation...
- Abandoned issues: often, perhaps in most cases, demands are not resolved upon the first contact with customers.
  - o The demands remain outstanding and afterwards someone has to handle them.
  - o A situation which can be very critical is when these demands are literally abandoned, neglected.

3.5. Handoffs

Handoffs can be understood to be "passing the baton", in situations of a process where a person or group must forward the process to another person or group, often outside the area or department itself. In support, the name given to this is scheduling.

A typical example of handoff is the one where support executes the assistance to the user, but is not responsible for resolving the issue. This is even very common: support executes the assistance, records the demand and is responsible for giving the return to the requestor. The person who resolves it, however, is in another area, and, unless appropriately informed about the context of the assistance, a lot of time can be wasted – or, even worse, there is a risk of annoying the customer asking things which were already asked in the first contact.

Due to the potential criticality, it is important to map these points, what they are and in which activities they are.

In the following table we present the hypothetical activities which we have mapped with the respective moments of truth, critical points and handoffs, also fictitious, but coherent with a real process, to illustrate the path taken so far.

Table 3.2. Activities, moments of truth, critical points and handoffs in a fictitious process in support

Activity	Moments of truth	Critical points	Handoffs
Start	-Ease of access to support -Availability of telephone or access by web portal -Information given by agent concerning rules and conditions of support	When agent has always to repeat the same questions to user about his environment	
Classifi-cation	Understanding of requestor's necessity		
Issue resolved?			

Yes-resolved	Issue can only be considered to be resolved if the user's requirement is really fulfilled Impression given to the customer that support tries "to free itself" from the call	Not resolve the issue within the deadline Does not escalate to the second level even being necessary Second level forgets to give assistance to user after being forwarded	Escalation from one level to another Escalation to another area to proceed with assistance
No – escalate level 2			
Resolve @ level 2			
Record resolution		Issue incorrectly recorded	
End		Close issue without resolution	

So far, we have only dealt with business process. Why? Let us remember that we want to deal with knowledge management aligned with business, so everything which we have done until now has been think about our business, right?

Afterwards, further on, this analysis will be able to be useful to evaluate if and in which way we could minimize the risks through good practices of creating knowledge content.

3.6. Measurement and monitoring of the process

Our process so far has its important items and activities defined and documented. Now we are going to try to define how we measure, or how we would like to measure this process.

Let us remember that, by definition, all the processes must have their performance measured.

It is necessary that we make an important distinction, which some people often fail to distinguish clearly. It concerns intrinsic indicators of the process and the indicators relevant to business. The concepts seem to be intermingled, but they have a subtle difference.

Once again, we are going to explain the concept with an example. Let us return to our support process and use as a reference the activity of escalating the issue for assistance by another area, when applicable (as we have already exemplified, in the cases where support does not resolve the demand at the first contact and forwards it to another area to act in the solution).

An indicator which could be created is the fulfillment of a deadline established for the issue to remain at each level. To ensure the performance of the process, it is rational to think of establishing a deadline so that the agent escalates for assistance by a specialized team at a higher level after some time is elapsed.

If we establish a deadline, we can want to measure the fulfillment of this deadline – this is natural and makes complete sense. This indicator is intrinsic to the process, because it can be fulfilled in 100% of the cases and even so the deadline for the process itself may not be being fulfilled.

This deadline for the process, agreed with the user, can indeed be a relevant indicator for business. The intrinsic indicators have their value, obviously, for analyzing the performance of the activities, performance of teams, etc. But for business what matters is total time spent at each instance of the process.

Another example, even more related to business: let us imagine a shared services area which is responsible for analyzing granting credit in a financial company.

The requests for credit are submitted and there is a process to analyze them, with the activities involved. In a case such as this, if we think about performance of the process, what is best for the company: having 100% of the analyses executed within the deadline established in the process or improving the quality of granting credit and thereby reducing the losses caused by default?

The two indicators are important, but with different target groups, or stakeholders.

The first one is more concerned with the direct authority for executing the activities of the process. The second one is related to business.

In the case of support, in many situations we have a support process, as it is not part of the end activity of the company. Except in cases where it is a services company or in cases like the one mentioned, of the financial area, in which the assistance is linked directly to business.

Whatever the case may be, we have to try to seek indicators aligned with business; if the process is one of support, it is necessary to seek something linked to the result of the area and its contribution to the business value chain.

To define appropriately what to measure, first we must think about the objective of the area or process. It may appear simple, and at the same time it may not be.

Let us then see if this is not the case.

If it is a services company and the end activity is rendering support services, then the support represents in itself only one process which is part of the core business.

Likewise for software companies, where the support aims to ensure the appropriate functioning of the software, which is the central business of the company. In these cases, the objective is always related to supporting the end activity of the business.

And if it is a support area in a company where the end activity is another one? The same reasoning is applied to shared services, which as a general rule render support services. How does one define the objective of the area, or of the processes of the area?

The objective must be related to supporting the business, ensuring the functioning of support areas without which the business itself would not be feasible.

Thinking about the objectives aims, in reality, to aid in defining the process indicators. To define the indicators, we have to think about what the company expects from the process or area. This is not easy, and unfortunately there is no ready-made recipe. Who to ask? And what do the users or customers expect from the area?

Regarding what users and customers expect, it is important to deal with a crucial issue, the expectations. In my first book (STATDLOBER, 2006) I looked at this issue of quality, at what rendering services with quality is. There is a certain distortion of conception in this respect, as there is a risk of simply assuming that rendering services with quality is doing it in the best way possible, or, in the generic form, "doing it with excellence", as indeed certain mission declarations are used to stating.

In fact, rendering services with quality is no more than fulfilling expectations, **which must be agreed beforehand in the so-called service level agreements (SLA).** The latter establish in a more or less detailed and formal manner what the rules and conditions are for any type of service rendered. Generally speaking, for the support processes, these rules are related to the deadlines, either for the start of the assistance or in certain cases even for the resolution.

Without agreements of this type, the user and the customer will always tend to have expectations of immediate solution, receipt of the service as quickly as possible, etc.

If this is ideal for the user, why then can we not mount a process to satisfy this type of expectation, let us say, immediate? Because we always have limited resources, whether human, technological, infrastructure or management.

What we can do is mount our process in accordance with a cost which we can bear.

Thus, when we define our indicators, their goals shall be aligned with the expectations agreed with users or customers. The most obvious example is, as was mentioned, regarding the deadlines. If we define as indicator the deadline for resolving issues, we have to place a goal – let us say, 90% of the issues resolved on time – which is known by everybody, executors of the process and users or customers.

Other examples of relevant indicators related to support perceived by customers are the solutions offered in the first assistance and the general perception of quality experienced by the customer. In the case of solutions of first assistance, there is a measure of efficacy of the assistance, generating at the same time a perception of "if I call, support resolves" by the users. The other item, the general perception of quality, can be measured by a satisfaction survey applied to support.

After all, why are we speaking about indicators and goals in a book which concerns knowledge management? First, because we want to think about knowledge management aligned with business and secondly because we want to implement knowledge management practices and then evaluate what benefit they may bring to business. These three metrics exemplified are extremely strong candidates to take as measurement for knowledge management.

As of now we are going to begin to deal with business management in practice properly speaking.

4. Preparation for Implementation of KM

As we have already mentioned previously in the first part of the book, during the conceptual foundation, and as the very practices guide of KCS mentions literally, "the concepts of KCS are simple, but adopting the methodology is not".

Any system, simple or complex, depends upon people.

By analyzing and understanding this statement, we can easily deduce that it is related to the human factor. How many of us have not experienced similar situations in the business world? A system or plan being implemented which ends up being forgotten, then languishing and finally dying... it is a very complex issue, which depends upon several critical factors, both on the side of the company which wants to adopt the system and on the side of the coworkers.

Some of these critical factors can invariably be defined by the following items.

It is certain that they represent critical factors, but they are not alone, as there can be others depending upon the reality of each company. Any of them can lead to lack of success in implementing the system.

On the side of the company

- **Real** willingness to adopt the system, with the **real** support of top management. The word real appears twice highlighted. It is necessary that the company really wants to implement knowledge management and that at least one top executive truly supports the initiative. What can the real involvement of a top executive be? An involvement of someone who knows the concepts well and really believes in the benefits. Many, many cases are already known, as in quality systems, for example, in which top management says that it supports it, but does not really get involved, does not know the subject and, underneath it all, only wants a certificate for marketing purposes.

- Availability of resources required. Supposing that the company and management really support it, resources must be made available. How can knowledge management be implemented without an appropriate tool? Conceptually, knowledge management and KCS assert that they are methodologies and that their focus must not refer to a tool. Clearly, but after everything is planned and ready to "run", it is impossible, in practice, to do it without a suitable tool.

- Prepared leadership. The leadership could also be listed on the side of the coworkers. Regardless of this theoretical classification, without good leaders a knowledge management system is not implemented. Good leaders, here, represent those people who manage to motivate, guide, correct and acknowledge the effort of their teams. Clearly they, before their teams, need to "buy the idea" and have the appropriate knowledge. They are the ones who will make the process proceed in the day-to-day, who must have perseverance to insist, to avoid entropy. And, if this occurs, that it is possible to identify the cause and act promptly.

On the side of the coworkers

- People committed to the company. We do not propose a utopian illusion with a rhetorical speech that all the coworkers are committed and fulfilled to the same extent, and that without this success is not achieved. But, on the other hand, we can state that if a certain area does not have some people with this characteristic, we shall not be successful.

Successful companies usually have some people who are more committed than others, who have more experience and knowledge, indeed, who are differentiated. These are the people that we need to count upon.

If we consider these items as being requirements, we can take them strongly into consideration for forming the pilot and planning group.

Another extremely important issue, perhaps the first practical recommendation for planning the implementation of a knowledge management system based upon KCS practices, is "begin small".

This, by the way, is a good practice in any new management system to be implemented in any company.

It is no use thinking of something on a very large scale, involving many areas and people, as there is a very great possibility of failure. The idea which we recommend, the same as KCS, incidentally, is to begin with a pilot program in one area, evaluate the evolution, learn, correct flaws, consolidate the system and only after this extend the scope to other areas. As already mentioned previously, the concepts of KCS are simple, but adopting the methodology is not.

There is no single action which ensures success in implementing the methodology.

We suggest, among others, activities as[1]:

- Definition of the area and team for the pilot study. As we have just said, there is no use in thinking about an initiative as being corporate, trying from the start to involve all the company. The recommendation is to choose a single area involved in customer assistance or technical support.

- Having defined the area, let us go the people. It is ideal to involve, besides the leaders, those people who stand out for initiative, interest and have advanced in their careers. All the area managers have clear the evaluation of these conditions in the group. Why not involve all the people in the area? It is very likely that a support area cannot remain without anybody providing operational assistance, and it cannot be received well by everybody to execute the activities proposed herein outside normal working hours. By the way, I think that this can even be a demotivating factor and generate resistance.

- Executive briefing and commitment of the people involved. First and foremost, people need to know and understand what they are going to be involved in. It is the moment to prepare an executive presentation about knowledge management and KCS, focusing upon the items which will be part of the process, explaining them, justifying them and whenever possible giving examples. We cannot think of somebody being committed or engaged without explaining the meaning

115

and context of things. Let us not forget that one of the benefits of adopting KCS is the improved satisfaction, motivation and self-esteem of people. We must aim to show this in the executive briefing.

- Planning meetings, as per the recommended roadmap of the topics to follow. The topics referred to are the ones which follow in this book, related to the study and documentation of data and information and definition of planning itself. For the development of the group activities which will be presented, known techniques can be used, like brainstorming or world café, a simple methodology, based upon seven principles, with techniques oriented towards group work (The World Café Community Foundation, http://www.theworldcafe.com/method.html).

- Training of people of the pilot area. At the end of the planning, before beginning to run the pilot study, obviously all the people in the area need to be trained

- Pilot study execution start.

[1] **Note**: as in all the scope of this work, I am presenting a roadmap suggested for implementing knowledge management based upon KCS practices, but not adopting them completely. Thus, the activities listed are the ones which I consider to be the most important. It should be borne in mind once again that this not a book which intends to implement KCS as a whole, but take as a basis its documented good practices and adapt them with

interpretations, synthesis and even my own recommendations.

5. Knowledge mapping

So far, we have managed to document reasonably well our support process with several important items for evaluation, including related to knowledge. As of this chapter we are going to begin to deal specifically with issues related to knowledge management.

We have had an excellent opportunity to think about our business, documenting our process. This was not done in vain, and now we are going to take a step forward.

As seen in the first part, in the chapter about knowledge management concepts, in organizations we have information and knowledge assets. What we propose here is to document what these assets are in each one of the activities of our support process, applying some of knowledge mapping concepts.

The breakdown of a process into activities greatly facilitates the study of these assets. Let us also remember the classification of the knowledge types (tacit and explicit). We are going to try to map all the knowledge, regardless of its classification.

As we have seen previously, tacit knowledge is the most complex to be mapped and documented. To do this thought by process can aid. What we do in each activity of the process can aid us in discovering which knowledge is desirable or necessary.

5.1. Mapping information and knowledge of a process

5.1.1. Preparation for mapping

The activities which will be proposed below will tend to be much more successful to the extent that we involve the people of the area. Perhaps you, as area manager, believe that you are capable of doing it alone, and you probably are. It is fundamental, however, not to fail to hear the people who take part in the process, the ones who are in touch with the users in the day-to-day. If it is not possible to hear them all, at least try to involve the greatest number of them possible. Often we hear very important suggestions from those in the front line.

At this first moment, the work has an approach related to the process of support and its requirements, it sufficing, therefore, to involve people from the support area. In the future, in analyzing the requirements studied, other areas shall probably take part, especially in processes where there occurs forwarding for solution by other areas – escalation. It is almost certain that part of the documentation necessary for the front line staff must be created by other specialized areas.

5.1.2. Executing the mapping

Given the diversity of environments, business and technologies handled, the examples become limited. But we are going to try to imagine some fictitious cases to try to drive thought in the case of each reader.

Document the data in a table like the one presented below, mapping the process, the knowledge required and the tacit and explicit knowledge used so far.

Certain considerations for filling in the table:

119

We are going to try, at this moment, not to be concerned yet with the conceptual differentiation between information or knowledge, which we saw in the first chapters. We are only going to try to make an inventory of **what it is necessary to know**, next to evaluate **what is in people's heads, what exists explicitly** and, then, **what we are lacking**.

[1] In the first column, 'Knowledge required', we are going to record the knowledge and information that we managed to remember which is important, and, therefore, required for the process. Seek to think about knowledge and information which are required, not only that which there is at the moment. This can be a good moment to discover what we are lacking. It is important to consider the day-to-day of the execution of the process, the daily operation. Thus, if certain knowledge required includes tacit or explicit information which you know exists, but in practice is not used, consider it to be nonexistent.

Do not worry at this moment in always finding a relationship between knowledge required and that which is tacit/explicit, as you may not find it. This, indeed, is one of the main objectives of the practice.

[2] In the column (Existing tacit knowledge) we are going to try to record the tacit knowledge which is required and that already is known by someone (what is in people's heads). In many cases, the knowledge required for a certain activity is part of the minimum skills required for a person to occupy a post and exercise his/her function, it sufficing, therefore, that there is only tacit knowledge. You can indicate this where it is applicable.

There may be situations where this applies, but you do not have anyone in the team with the skills required. Mark this as well, as **it can indicate that you need a new person in the team** or that it is necessary to train someone in the current team to obtain this knowledge, or, also, resolve this lack with explicit knowledge.

[3] In the third column (Existing explicit knowledge) we are going to list the explicit knowledge **which is required and that already exists, and which, therefore, is used**.

By exclusion, we shall arrive at the explicit knowledge that we do not have. If a report is considered to be necessary, it suffices that it is mentioned what it is. The most important is that it is recorded in a language which everyone understands clearly and afterwards remember exactly what it refers to.

Where knowledge required does not have corresponding tacit or explicit knowledge, mark only an X.

If tacit knowledge is sufficient, and corresponding explicit knowledge is not relevant, we suggest marking it with NA (not applicable).

Be careful with the definition of not applicable, as you may be determining that you will not need any type of explicit documentation without a deeper analysis.

Note

> This is one of the most important points in all the practice of knowledge management. Appropriate time and conditions must be expended to study these items. They are fundamental for a suitable knowledge management approach.

Below there is a hypothetical example of a support process which assists its customers with and without contract, in networks, Internet and infrastructure.

Table 5.1. Mapping knowledge of a process

[1] Knowledge required	[2] Existing tacit knowledge	[3] Existing explicit knowledge	Remarks
Use of help desk software	Everyone is trained when joining the company	NA	
History of all issues		Report in help desk software	
Knowledge on networks and internet	It is part of the requirements for employees to be hired		
TCP/IP routing rules	X		We do not have a professional with this knowledge, although it is fundamental
Firewall security rules	Knowledge related to the function of the hired analyst		
Customer environment, architecture and topology	X	X	

Contractual conditions, validity, number of hours contracted, etc.	X	Spreadsheet of contracts and assistance conditions	

Now that we have more clearly defined what the knowledge assets are related to our support process, we can improve and make more profound the documentation, relating it to the attributions (roles) of the people, the knowledge that these people need to have to perform their attributions, the analysis of criticality of the explicit and tacit assets as well as the identification of holders of tacit knowledge.

5.2. Matrix of explicit knowledge – attributions, knowledge required and criticality

Each knowledge asset mapped as explicit in Table 5.1-column [3], can now be related to the attributions of the people who interact with it (the asset) during the execution of the process – i.e., which people, through the respective roles which they perform, use these explicit assets. Furthermore, we are going to analyze and classify these assets regarding their criticality.

The objective is to relate the functions which people perform (attributions or roles) to the assets which they use, and also evaluate how critical each one of the assets is.

Table 5.2. Explicit knowledge – attributions, criticality and knowledge required

Explicit knowledge	Criticality 1-Low, 2-Medium, 3-High	Attributions
History of all issues	2	All agents
Contractual conditions, validity, number of hours contracted, etc.	3	All people from support

5.3. Matrix of tacit knowledge – holders of knowledge and criticality

For those items classified as 'existing tacit knowledge' (Table 5.1- column [2]), we are going to define their criticality for the process and who are the people that hold them. We are going to name people individually or groups.

Table 5.3. Tacit knowledge, criticality and holders of knowledge

Tacit knowledge	Criticality 1-Low, 2-Medium, 3-High	People
Use of help desk software	1	All
Knowledge on networks and internet	2	All
Firewall security rules	3	John

Alert: warning point identified!

In an example like this, we have already clearly identified a warning point. In the area of knowledge of 'Firewall security rules' **we have only one person with tacit knowledge in a high criticality point**. As it is tacit knowledge, we depend upon people, and in this case one only. If he leaves the organization, we will be without knowledge in this area.

Situations like this deserve a special action plan!

5.4. Explicit knowledge gaps

Taking again as basis the knowledge by process which we have already mapped, we can now concentrate on explicit knowledge gaps, i.e., on that explicit knowledge which is desirable or necessary. We can also take advantage of it and analyze if the explicit knowledge which we have currently is appropriate and satisfactory.

We are going to repeat the items of Table 5.1 in the following table, first executing an analysis to determine if the existing explicit knowledge is satisfactory (column '**Existing content analysis**'). It is an opportunity to analyze the quality and utility of the current explicit knowledge.

For the knowledge which is necessary and that does not have related explicit knowledge, first we are going to analyze if it would be really relevant to have it and, in this case, what would be suitable to document (column '**Required content analysis**).

Seek to document in the most detailed and didactic manner possible that which would be ideal to have documented. Specify product or software, version, context, indeed, everything which is relevant.

Table 5.4. Explicit knowledge gaps

Information / knowledge required	Existing explicit knowledge /information	Existing content analysis	Required content analysis
Use of help desk software	NA		
History of all issues	Report in help desk software	Partially satisfactory. It would be ideal to have in the listing access to the history of assistance executed	The access should be easier for accessing the system
Knowledge on networks and internet	X		It is not necessary as it is basic knowledge of the function which the analysts exercise
TCP/IP routing rules	X		It would be ideal to have documentation about concepts and how to

			configure routing in Windows 7 and Linux
Firewall security rules	X		Security rules for firewalls Fsec and X-block would help; a large part of the customers use these products and need new rules periodically
Customer environment, architecture and topology	X		It is fundamental to know which software versions the customers use
Contractual conditions, validity, number of hours contracted, etc.	Spreadsheet of contracts and assistance conditions	We always have to look at the spreadsheet, which is often out-of-date. We have problems, as often we attend customers without a contract or with the call	

		number of the month finished, which should not be the case	

In the analyses made so far, we have managed to identify:

- A warning point referring to a knowledge area where we have only one person in the company who masters it.
- Five knowledge areas which require documentation actions:
    - o Two of them are improvements (access to the history of all issues and access and integrity of the contract data).
    - o Three with documentation to be created, referring to routing rules, security rules and software versions which the customers use.

5.5. Proactive knowledge management

Before proceeding with the planning, we need to formalize these holdovers detected and define how we shall resolve them. Even being in the planning phase, we need to have a plan to resolve these items, after all, if our analysis was correct, it is information and knowledge required for our process.

Hence, **we are putting into practice proactive knowledge management** – which was mentioned in the first chapter of this book.

The suggestion is that the actions are formalized, with their assignments and preferably with terms. The control can be simple, but it is necessary that it is clear regarding what needs to be done, by whom and in which term.

A suggested action plan, based upon these items, can be viewed in the following table. It is clear that this table is a simplified representation. The items to be created could be more detailed, as the technological complexity can be very great, probably involving several specialists.

The most important is to leave a recommendation and an example that, at the point at which we have reached, it is fundamental to deal with the shortcomings detected as holdovers and that they are not left aside.

Table 5.5. Content creation action plan

Item	Assignee	Due date
Make available history of all issues of software X		
Online access to contract data		
Create technical documentation about security rules		
Create technical documentation about firewall rules		
Evaluate feasibility and create environment for documentation of customer environments		

5.6. Knowledge collected during the execution of processes

Before starting this topic, a clarification is important. We are going to deal with an item which is not explicitly part of the concepts of KCS and also is not traditionally looked at by BPM.

It is, in a certain way, an innovating approach, as it joins together process management and knowledge management.

As we have already contextualized, the processes have their stages and activities, which are executed inside the support area or forwarded to other areas. We have issues with deadlines, escalations, as well as handoffs.

It can never be stressed enough that, in practice, it is frequently observed that the deadlines and handoffs can be critical for the progress of the process itself, so that we classified them in the previous exercise as critical points (Table 3.2).

What we want to evaluate now is which opportunities of knowledge generation we can have, or rather, we can plan, in these events of the processes.

Is it confusing, dear reader? Let us return to the examples.

Let us look at a hypothetical situation in which the first level agent deals with a problem of the user and who, after diagnosis, concludes that it is a problem in the database. In such cases the issue is escalated to the infrastructure area, with the DBAs, who are specialists in this area of knowledge.

For cases like this, I am sure that there are opportunities of creating explicit knowledge, starting from the perspective of the context of the person who executes the first assistance and sends the issue ahead. In the day-to-day of support we encounter such situations, in which **the issue returns back to the first level without having taken advantage of the opportunity of creating documentation at higher levels**.

One of the basic assumptions of KCS is to make use of the user's context to create explicit knowledge, only that, in cases like this, the context is obtained at the initial level of the assistance, and the higher level analyst, who receives the issue, makes a technical intervention of assistance away from the customer.

How can this be dealt with?

Depending upon the software tool which is used to control knowledge management and support, ideally certain rules of requirements of creating explicit knowledge are bound to the process activities. For example, one of the ways of resolving this could be only allow the escalation of the issue if an article with the user's context and symptoms is created. In the next level, where the specialized assistance occurs, there would be another similar control which only allowed the "return" of the issue to the previous level if the DBA analyst made an update in the article created previously. This update could be executed completing the article which was created in the previous level or it could be a comment or observation, which would be consolidated by the technical reviewer of the article type. This is no more than collaboration, only it is controlled by process rules.

There are situations where this practice can be even more beneficial.

Let us imagine the scenario of support to software users, done by a development company. In a first occurrence of a certain software failure, there occurs the escalation to the software development area for correction. The update of the article, for the context of the problem, will indicate that the correction was applied in a determined release of the software. In the case of a new report of the same problem, in the same context, the agent of the first level could already give the solution directly, sending the release which corrects that problem (search early, search often).

The adoption of this practice would result, therefore, in some very clear benefits:

- Construction of collaborative knowledge ensured by execution rules of the process. Without there being the collaboration for the construction of knowledge, the process simply "locks".
- From the point of view of the assistance itself, knowledge would have been obtained in an appropriate manner. In another occurrence of the same problem, or

133

a similar one, any agent would know which solution was applied, reducing the time spent in diagnosis.

5.7. Definition of information for end users or customers

So far, we have thought about our support process and the information and knowledge existing or required, from our point of view as attendants of the processes.

It is appropriate for us to reflect also from the point of view of the users or customers.

As we are in direct contact with them, it is likely that we can think about their recurring requirements, which may be able to be handled with directed information.

Specific user information must be dealt with in this way because the interest and understanding of language are different. The type of information which a user requires will probably differ from the type which the attending technician is used to.

The language, equally, must be compatible with somebody who is not a specialized technician in IT or technical areas of a process.

If you, reader, call your operator because there is a problem related to your cable TV package, which of the following languages would be most appropriate and understandable?

— [Customer] "I have a problem with my TV, no channel is functioning".

— [Agent, scenario 1] "Sir, please disconnect your set top box from the socket, wait

a minute and then connect it again".

— [Agent, scenario 2] "Sir, the firmware may be frozen by oscillation of

alternate energy in transistor. Ideally, cut the supply and execute a hard-reset".

The difference in language could be understood, could it not? Even though it is a bit of an exaggerated example, I believe that the question of language has been left clear.

The format of the information made available can vary, depending upon the resources that can be used. A good resource, to facilitate and guide users, is the offer of self-service, either by categorized access to the information or by the use of assistance scripts – both valid for the case of offering support by Web portal.

The scripts are a roadmap with a set of questions with alternatives; to the extent that the user navigates in the script, signaling alternatives, questions related to the previous answers are presented.

During the navigation of the user by the script, relevant information can be presented, as documents or contents of instructions, for example.

At the end, if the user has not managed to resolve his/her requirement, a demand will be generated with history of the path taken in the user's navigation in the script, which can be used to aid in assistance.

Another way often used to offer contents to the users, rather efficacious, by the way, is making frequently asked questions - FAQ available. The challenge lies in defining and publishing items which really are frequent problems or queries of users or customers (we shall see how to deal with this further on), and in displaying it in a direct and clear manner. Ideally short, succinct descriptions are used and the results presented in an equally direct and objective format.

Although the examples mentioned are not specifically of IT, I believe that they have served to clarify the concepts.

The study of user requirements is relatively simple. It concerns a listing of items which are important to customers, with their description and the benefit expected. Perhaps you already offer some information required to your users; in this case, mark this in the last column.

Below there is an example of certain information which could be relevant to customers in a technical support process in companies of IT services.

Table 5.6. Study of possible requirements of users or customers

Item	Description	Expected benefit	Existing?
Information about contract conditions	Information about validity, price, agreements and rights (assistance terms and conditions), etc.	Customer knows clearly the time conditions for solutions, terms for assistance, etc.	N
Basic diagnostic tips, style "frequently asked questions"	List of frequently asked questions, easy to access and understand	Customers could resolve the simplest doubts without needing to await assistance or make calls to support	N
Information about demands in assistance	List of open and closed demands	Customer does not need to call the help desk to know the progress of his/her demands	S

Note

A practice which can be recommended is to publish information to the users so that the articles most accessed appear highlighted, something like "Top 10", making the ten articles most accessed appear in first place. Finally we have an aid so that our knowledge management planning can advance and begin to be formalized.

Let us remember that so far we have mapped critical points, information lacking or nonexistent which are relevant to our process and we have also defined certain information which we believe to be useful to our users or customers.

6. Review and Definition of Monitoring Items

6.1. Support Process oriented Indicators

However strange it may appear at first sight, it is advisable for us to begin by defining the monitoring items, as we must execute some of the measurements and have data about them before implementing any knowledge management practice.

This basically applies to the performance indicators oriented towards support process and aims to obtain base data for comparison, which is called baseline. It is essential that we have the indicators before and after implementing knowledge management practices, so that we can evaluate with clarity the results obtained, through the analysis of evolution of these indicators.

As per the topic "Measurement and monitoring of the process", of Chapter 3, for assistance in support or customer care, at least four relevant measurements would be:

- Fulfillment of deadlines for demands (AKA SLA fulfillment).
- Number of demands resolved in first contact.
- Average resolution time of demands.
- Perception of user satisfaction.

Considering these measurements, we would arrive at the following table:

Table 6.1. Definition of business oriented indicators

Indicator	Description	Goal
SLA fulfillment	Percentage of demands resolved within agreed SLA	>=80%
First Call Resolution (FCR)*	Percentage of demands resolved in the first contact with the user or customer	>=30%
Average resolution time	Average resolution time of demands	
User satisfaction	Percentage of evaluations concerning assistance with positive perception	>=85%

* **FCR** is an acronym used for this type of measurement: First Call Resolution.

It is very important here that you manage to think if in your company there is any other type of indicator to be considered, in the same line as these, which are relevant to business. Try to evaluate the possibility of collecting these indicators by issue type, grouping the ones with similar features – not losing sight of the perspectives of customers, coworkers and the organization.

If your company has as end activity the rendering of services, you may perhaps monitor customer loyalty and default, for example, if considering that ready and efficacious assistance helps to maintain the customer base.

In shared services, perhaps a good assistance provided by your area impacts on business indicators of other areas. In this case, ideally your assistance indicators would be made to affect the indicators of the customer area, in a concept of BSC – balanced scorecard.

Having defined the business indicators, it is fundamental that you manage to execute the monitoring and collection of results. After beginning to implement practices of knowledge management, you will be able to follow up the Evolution trend of your results.

Important note

> When the group is gathered together discussing indicators, during the discussion dynamics, conclusions can arise concerning certain critical points which stand out from the others, those main elements which would represent gains if handled appropriately.
>
> Be attentive, as it can be an excellent opportunity to detect or formalize them.

6.2. Indicators Related to Knowledge Management

Having defined the indicators related to support process, and considering that baseline measurements begin to be taken, we can now plan which indicators related to knowledge management will be part of our system.

Generally speaking, we can regard our knowledge management system as a set of information which will be created, maintained updated, transmitted and "consumed" to in some way improve our support process.

As rather well developed in Practice 7, "Performance evaluation", Technique 3, "balanced scorecard", of the evolve loop, ideally one thinks of a set of indicators which links individual goals and measurements to those of the group. It is also worth bearing in mind that the issue of quality of the articles is dealt with in Practice 5, "Content Health", Technique 4, "Quality management of articles".

Also in accordance with the precepts of KCS, all the participants end up becoming responsible for generating information and, consequently, knowledge. It is important to evaluate the production of contents both from the quantitative point of view, related to the number of articles created, and related to the quality of the content.

Whether related to quantity or quality, it is advisable to start with a reasonably small number of indicators, so that, later, with the maturity of the system, they are reviewed – or new indicators are created.

Certain measurements which can be suggested and that are relevant to any knowledge management initiative are listed below.

Regarding the quantity of content produced:

- Articles created by the author.
- Articles reviewed: considering review to be direct update of content or request for review – remember the concepts that each reponder is responsible for the content which (s)he accesses and the concept 'flag it or fix it'. The action of reviewing or requesting review is positive, as it indicates initiative and proactivity in the sense of maintaining the knowledge base updated.
- Optionally, both items can be measured for groups.
- Number of articles made available for customers.

Regarding the quality of content produced, the following could be measured, for example:

- Number of incidents resolved with the support of articles existing previously: it represents the measurement of one of the main objectives of KCS, which is that of using explicit knowledge to aid in resolving issues. See more details about this item in the topic concerning audits, further on.
- Number of displays of articles with positive evaluation of utility by author: quantity of articles used and evaluated as "useful", representing efficacy of content created; preferably separating agents and customer evaluations.
- Number of searches made which lead to outstanding documentation or creation of new articles – knowledge gap –, measuring documentation lacking.
- Number of customer accesses to articles: a measure of use of information by customers, including facility of localization of information.
- Number of observations indicated in audits referring to content quality.

Several other measurements can be created, but, as we mentioned previously, a good practice is to begin with a number not so large, to evaluate later the real requirement of new indicators.

As a recommendation, the indicators listed can be sufficient to begin the work.

Important note

Goals of knowledge management indicators
As mentioned in the technique related to the balanced scorecard, in the practices guide of KCS, it is coherent that these indicators are created without goals, as above all it is people's commitment that is sought and it is hoped that, thus, they collaborate spontaneously.

> Furthermore, it is collaboration of an intellectual nature, and perhaps goals force a production of quantity without quality – production to fulfill goals.

Both in KCS and in any other methodology or set of practices, it is up to each one to analyze and decide about following or not, at risk, the recommendations. I, particularly, am in favor of this idea, at least at first as we want to sensitize and motivate people. If we are successful in this, it is not the goals which would make a difference in productivity.

With the measurements mentioned, we arrive at our indicators.

Table 7.1. Indicators of knowledge management

Indicator	Description
Quantitative	
# Articles created by author	Quantity of articles created by author
# Articles reviewed by author	Quantity of reviews executed or requested by reviewer
# Articles made available for customers by author	Quantity of articles published and made available for customers as per rules of structuring, classification, etc.
Qualitative	
# Incidents resolved with existing articles (known)	Quantity of incidents resolved using preexisting documentation
% Known / new	Percentage of incidents resolved with use of preexisting documentation related to the total of incidents resolved
# Positive evaluations by author	Quantity of evaluations of articles as "useful", by author
# Searches for knowledge gap by area	Searches by content resulting in nonexistent articles
# Customer accesses by author	Quantity of exhibitions of articles by customers, by author
# Audit findings	Number of findings related to quality of content, by author

At the point of the planning where we are, we have defined, therefore, the knowledge management indicators which will be measured.

As can be observed, the indicators are related to the efficiency and efficacy of people. Even without goals, we need spontaneous adhesion and the proactive participation of people. It is important to define how to work on these results, how to use them to engage the participation of everybody. Further on we are going to deal specifically with this issue.

Note

Obviously at this point you must be concluding that it is necessary to think about how to operationalize all this system, requiring evaluating the use of a software tool. It is even possible to adopt these practices manually, but the effort spent may make the project unfeasible.

Both knowledge management and KCS itself assert that the implementation depends upon factors of motivation, management and focus, but, in the end, without a tool, without software, the result becomes unfeasible in practice.

7. Structuring of Knowledge Base

The structuring concerns the manner in which the information, knowledge or, in the last analysis, the articles are obtained and stored.

The importance of appropriate planning of this issue can never be stressed too much.

It will determine not only which information will be documented in the articles, but also the organization of this storage. The more appropriate the structuring, the better the conditions which will be given to recovery.

In our planning of structuring, we need to take into account at least the following elements:

- Types of article.
- Attributes of information.
- Good Documentation Practices.
- Storage structure.
- Model of publication/update.

We shall see below more details about each one of them.

7.1. Types of articles

In a taxonomy approach, the type of article represents the first level of classification. It corresponds to a first grouping, placing in the same set similar articles of objectives or "reasons for existing".

As they have similar features, rules of permissions and behavior can also be defined by types of articles, such as, for example, definition of authors and reviewers and model of publication – to be explained in the following item.

Examples of types of article which could be adopted:

- Failures and error.
- Technical specifications.
- Business rules.
- Standards and procedures.
- Frequently asked questions.
- Technical instructions.

As certain of these items will be defined by type of article and require greater clarification, we shall construct our table of types and other attributes in sequence.

7.2. Attributes of information

The attributes represent the types of information desirable to store in the knowledge base. As we are using a grouping of articles by type, it is coherent for us to think that articles of the same type have similar attributes, while those belonging to different types may have other common information with each other.

Thus, we can specify obtaining information attributes as per each type of article.

Remembering the concepts of KCS, their practices recommend that there are at least the following mandatory attributes:

- Description.
- Symptom or problem.
- Customer's context.
- Environment.
- Cause.
- Solution applied.

Note

These attributes suggested refer exclusively to articles related to resolving incidents or problems. Other types of article would have reasons to use other attributes. For articles related to software failures, for example, instead of a generic attribute for environment, version and release of

> software used and date of installation could be documented, for example.

Certain other information can be useful regardless of the type of article, such as, for example, tags or keywords, which would also be used in searches.

The concept of tags is commonly adopted in blogs and other publications on the Internet. They serve as an additional level of identification for use and later in searches.

KCS also suggests the use of metadata, which is general information related to control, like date/time of creation and update of articles, information about evaluation of utility and number of exhibitions, for example. This type of information depends above all upon its availability in the tool which will be used.

Important note

> An important type of metadata to be stored with the article, according to the recommendation of KCS, is the set of search arguments used to display each article.

7.3. Good Documentation Practices

Having defined the attributes which will be recorded for each type of article, ideally certain norms and standards should be created, related to how the contents will be written. If on one hand a standard can limit creativity, it is fundamental so that the result produced by different people has a certain uniformity. We do not want to restrict the process, but try to have a certain coherence of language to facilitate the search for information and understanding. Anyway, we prefer to call this document guide, and not standard.

The guide will probably have reviews and be modified over time. But I believe that it is important to begin with some definitions, albeit simple ones. What type of definitions are we talking about, after all?

We can suggest certain definitions, such as the ones listed below.

Table 7.2. Suggested Good Documentation Practices

1. In the description of fact or symptom: use short phrases, which report the fact.		
	1.1	If it is a problem, describe it in a direct manner, using expressions like "is unable to...", "Problem in..." or "[resource] does not function...".
	1.2	If it is a customer doubt, use a question in the shortest form possible.
2. Try to put in the description, if possible, the environment or context, explaining where the problem occurs.		
3. Try to remove words which do not add information useful to the fact.		
4. Avoid long paragraphs, except when strictly necessary.		
5. In the case of description of solution, try whenever possible to enumerate steps in lists or with the use of bullets.		
6. Avoid the gerund and write a symptom, cause, fact, etc. in the clearest way possible.		
7. Never use contents of emails pasted directly in any documentation.		

As important as the items of the guide would be to create an annex with examples of how to do and not do things – the so-called "**examples and non-examples**". Nothing like good examples to make things clear!

The complement of our good documentation practices could be as per the following table:

Table 7.3. Examples and non-examples of the suggestions guide

Item	Examples	Non-examples
	-Unable to send and receive emails -Problem in sending and receiving emails	Customer reports that (s)he accessed Outlook and upon clicking on the send button remained with the messages trapped in the outbox and also found that new messages are not appearing in the inbox
	-Unable to send and receive emails in the notebook -Problem in sending and receiving emails in the notebook	Customer reports that (s)he accessed Outlook in the notebook and upon clicking on the send button remained with the messages trapped in the outbox and also found that new messages are not appearing in the inbox. (S)he finds it strange that in his/her desktop computer everything functions
	-Loss of connection with the server	<From: joao@servidor.com.br> <Subject: problem in the network> <content-type> ...., etc., etc.
	-How to change the severity of a requisition in the Web portal?	Customer called and alleges that (s)he is unable to change the severity of a requisition made by the Web portal yesterday

151

Observations about the items:

Item 1: however many details are described in the third column, what is really relevant in this case is that (s)he is unable to send or receive emails. This can, however, have an important feature referring to the environment, which must be obtained. See item 2.

Item 2: an essential item of information was obtained, that the problem occurs in the notebook. In this case it is more important than ever to obtain information about the environment. But it could be better... what system is there in the notebook? What software? The details about the environment do not need to be in the description of the problem, they could be in an environment attribute.

Item 3: it is extremely time consuming to locate information in email contents. If it is inevitable to paste content, remove everything which is not information relevant to the context.

Item 4: perceive the clarity in the definition on the left compared with on the right, which requires a more detailed reading to understand it.

The good documentation practices and its annex are only one example. It is strongly recommended that the guide of your company is developed in group work, with the participation of the greatest number possible of people who are involved in creating content and searching for it.

After being defined, the guide must be made available and easily accessed by everyone at any moment during their work.

7.4. Storage structure

The storage structure to be defined is a hierarchical filing organization, equivalent to the folders of Windows files.

It concerns a quite usual method of classifying for storage, adopted even in non-electronic systems, as drawers with foldable files or in libraries (sections, stands, shelves, etc.). We are also speaking about those metal cabinets, with their pull-outs, remember? We have in the drawer a label which indicates what is contained in it, such as customers, for example. Upon opening the drawer, there are foldable files with small ID labels, usually the customer's name. Inside the file, there may be envelopes with similar papers, as contracts and invoices. There we have a physical example of three storage levels.

In our planning, we can define files and sub-files, in as many levels as appropriate. There is no rule, but generally more than three levels tends to make the classification very subjective.

The relationships between types of article and folders at first can generate a certain doubt, to be able to represent similar groupings. One suggestion would be to use folders to separate the types of article into more specific level. There is no right or wrong model, the one most suited to each organization being valid.

An interesting approach is to use the structure of folders to define the permissions of access or viewing of content. The concept would be coherent as articles of determined types are stored together in folders.

It is also possible to define segmentation between contents for agents and users or customers, through folders viewed only by them (as is the case, in practice, of a file for "frequently asked questions", for example).

The following table shows a hypothetical storage structure which could be defined, presented only to illustrate the concept of files and sub-files.

Table 7.3. Example of file structure for storage

1. Technical specifications			
	1.1	Software X	
		1.1.1	Version 1.0
		1.1.2	Version 2.0
	1.2	Software Y	
2. Operating procedures			
	2.1	Access validation	
	2.1	Security compliance	

7.5. Model of publication/update

Although KCS presents as premise the constant update of information during its use, or at least the indication that information requires updating (fix it or flag it), there can be situations where it is not desirable or is not feasible to allow these updates in a decentralized manner, or at least without a centralized reviewing control.

One scenario for this situation is the case of information concerning organizational policies and standards, for example. It is important and necessary to publish them and make them accessible to those for whom access is relevant, but is very unlikely that a company releases reviews and updates of this type of document to be done by several people, indiscriminately.

Think, reader, about standards of travel or vacation prepayments, for example. In your company, would the update model be similar to that which KCS advocates, with updates allowed in a decentralized manner? I believe not. Clearly, we have to consider that knowledge articles and standards have different uses.

Even in dealing with documentation of articles, there can be similar situations.

Some type of information which will be made available to aid in diagnosing and resolving critical problems may need to have its update centralized.

Imagine an area of customer service to life support appliances in the medical area. It would be more coherent that the assistance instructions are only written and reviewed by people with deep knowledge in the subject. Ideally this model should be defined by article type.

Certain definitions required, regarding these permissions, which could be defined by type of article:

- Permission of direct update of articles published by responders with attribution of author.
- Review permissions.

These permissions would be delegated to people with the due qualification.

8. Definition of Responsibilities

This item of our planning concerns "who will do what" in our knowledge management system. In a previous topic (6.2) mention was made of adopting or not goals for certain indicators. In that case, we resolved to follow at risk the recommendations.

Regarding attributions and responsibilities, however, we are going to propose a model a little more simplified than the guide suggests. In the case of KCS, and also in other disciplines, such as ITIL, for example, very broad responsibility attributions are recommended, devised to be adopted in cases where many people are available to perform in the processes. Often, in practice, there is not the number of people available for each attribution, and in these cases it is advisable to accumulate responsibilities and functions in certain people.

I believe that we can begin the implementation of knowledge management with attributions and functions adapted to our reality, in a slightly more simplified manner.

I propose adopting the roles listed below.

I remind you that attributions are roles – and that, therefore, they can be performed by people in common (more than one attribution exercised by one person, for example).

- Leader: (s)he will be responsible for conducting the implementation at the broadest level, management, controlling the activities required for the planning, implementation and maintenance of the system. It is advisable that the leader has profound knowledge in KCS so that (s)he can aid in general issues related to the system as a whole.

- Mentor: a mentor can be considered to be a leader who focuses more on the process, the execution, the day-to-day. It is highly advisable that the mentor has wide knowledge of KCS. The mentor's skills must include a good relationship with people, being a motivator and having aptitude to take correction measures which are required.
- Author: as the name indicates, it is the attribution which determines the qualification and permission to write new articles. As seen previously, there can be situations where the creation of articles must be restricted for security reasons or to allow that only specialists write certain types of article – in the cases where the specialization requirements are high and the articles need to have reliable contents, i.e., they are of high criticality. Anyway, it is advisable to define authors by article type, and that they are very knowledgeable in their respective area.
- Reviewers: they are users who can execute updates in articles, maintaining the same conditions mentioned previously for authors.

Important note

Although not mentioned as an attribution, it is worth bearing in mind that **it is fundamental that there is a supporter of top management**, who is a high executive in the company. Further on, when the system is implemented and operational, you will need the involvement of this high executive in the critical analysis of the system. We shall look at this issue later on in this book, when we are following up knowledge management, after the system has begun to "run".

9. Account Profiles and Customer Configurations

Besides all the documentation which we have dealt with so far, when executing assistance it is important to know the user or customer that we are attending.

If we return to the chapter which deals with the attributes of information (7.2), we can see that one of these attributes concerns exactly the environment in which the problem (or the requirement) occurs. The context which it is proposed to search, in this item, is related to information concerning customers on two fronts. It is worth emphasizing that, as presented in the chapter of concepts about KCS, these items are considered to be knowledge assets, but they are not focused on in the current version of KCS. The practices guide itself indicates that in ensuing versions they will be incorporated in a more detailed manner.

We can, however, regardless of the KCS practices guide, see value in this information and try to use it. In the case of account profiles, the importance occurs especially for companies where assistance is executed for external customers or users.

9.1. Account profiles

Account profiles concern every type of information of a commercial relationship between the support area and the user or customer. We can think about naming this resource as "customer profiles".

We take as first scenario an IT company which renders support services to its customers. The account profiles would be very useful with the following examples of information attributes:

- Existing contract(s).
- Contractual validities.
- Contractual conditions.
- Contract consumption: in many cases, contracts have limitations, by number of hours, number of incidents, etc.
- Payments made or due: in the case of outstanding payment, for example, there can be a policy which determines that services cannot be rendered until the situation has been regularized.

Another scenario which we can illustrate is that of assistance to users of a certain subscription service. It can be a company which renders ticket service in tolls and parking lots, of which the support area executes assistance to customers who are users of the automatic payment chip.

In this type of scenario, the account profile would have information such as:

- Service or plan contracted.
- Collection type: if it is a pre- or post-paid plan.
- Consumption so far: hypothetically, how many tickets already used in the month and what the owed balance of the period is.
- History of payments made.
- Outstanding payments.

We have had two examples and could have countless others. The most important is not to pay attention to the examples specifically, but to the assumptions that:

- This information is important for assistance and, therefore, must be part of our knowledge base.
- Different to what we have been constructing so far, some of this information (that related to consumption, for example) is not static. Therefore, a manual registration and update model becomes practically unfeasible. This type of situation requires an integration of systems, with access routines or gateways.

Our challenge at this moment of planning is, first, identify which information the support process requires. Then, we need to define how to obtain it.

It is certain that it already exists in the company, in financial, corporate ERP systems or even some things in other sources, such as spreadsheets. What we need to do is define how we shall give the agents access to this information.

One way, more obvious and apparently simple, is to give the agents access to the systems of the information origin. Think hard before following this path, as it has certain disadvantages:

- Complexity: the information required may be in more than one module of an ERP system or, worse, in more than one system. This increases the complexity of granting access, training agents (who need to know more than one system/module) and makes it more difficult to use – in practice, people work with several windows open at the same time).
- Self-help for customers: do you remember, dear reader, that previously we looked at the issue of information made available to users or customers, enabling them to resolve their requirements with self-help? Well, the use of legacy systems with access by the end-users prevents any initiative in this respect. Obviously, we cannot

offer customers access to the legacy systems of the company!

So, what can be done?

Suppose that you have done your part in planning the information, defining and validating attributes of account profiles which are really important and desirable for assistance.

Above all, you need the tool to handle integration with other legacy systems. If you are lucky and your tool handles integration, the moment has come to work with the systems area, or IT, to define an integration project.

It is advisable that this integration allows access to information required in the most friendly way possible, preferably on the same screen where the issue is being recorded, and whenever making use of the context of the assistance being executed – at that moment you probably needed to identify the customer. So, nothing more natural than searching for information of account profile with a function being executed on the agent's assistance screen itself.

9.2. Customer configurations

It is information of a more technical nature, related to the customer's environment. In the case of assistance in IT, it can contain the description of the environment, its architecture, software and products installed, indeed, everything which is important to aid in the diagnosis or to facilitate the execution of services.

In theory, at some moment someone had contact with the customer's environment, directly or indirectly. At least in a previous assistance a technician was in contact with a

161

component of the customer's environment. It is advisable that the configuration information of customers is registered previously and is available as soon as the assistance is executed. In the case of service companies, a good moment is straight after the closing of the contract. Ideally in this case one should try to document the environment of customers before beginning any assistance.

During the assistance itself, the configuration information of customers must be updated as soon as any alteration is detected.

This type of documentation impacts directly on the customer's perception regarding the quality of the assistance, including being part of a magical moment (take advantage of it and have another look, if you deem it necessary, at the topic concerning moments of truth [3.3] and their critical points [3.4]).

As we have done in the other items of our planning of knowledge management, we need to define the information attributes which we want to document regarding customer configurations.

10. Definition of Quality Audit System

Any system implemented which is based upon continuous improvement has a stage related to the *Check* of PDCA – this stage which is related to checking how the things are being done, based upon the planning executed. As perceived, the double loop process of KCS is nothing more than an adapted vision of an implementation of the PDCA cycle.

In this chapter we are going to look precisely at the planning of checking the process already in execution. In other words, we can state that we aim at planning an audit system.

The KCS practice related to what we are dealing with is 5, Content Health, of the evolve loop. Certain techniques refer to concepts related to the subject. In the development of our planning, we have already analyzed and defined indicators which will be used to monitor our process.

Generally speaking, the indicators represent a good part of the check which we can execute in our process. In the manner that they are defined, our qualitative indicators allow us to infer if the quality of the articles is good, given their practical use. This does not indicate, however, that more profound analyses cannot be done to aid in checking the efficacy of our system and, possibly, if necessary, generating improvement actions.

10.1. Known x new

One of the most important items for KCS is resolving incidents through using articles which already existed before assistance. These existing articles, used in resolving incidents are called "**known**", meaning that the solution for an issue was known, and this solution was documented explicitly. On the other hand, in the cases in which a solution is not documented and it is created just-in-time when dealing with an issue, the term used is "**new**". The link of an incident resolved with a previously existing article is called, in the original literature of KCS, '**incident link**'. We are going to use the expression "incident link",or simply the word "**link**".

A good knowledge base, well designed and constantly updated, tends to increase the number of incidents resolved using knowledge previously documented and, therefore, **known**. In the planning of indicators, we have already defined a metric to monitor this item. So, what else can we do about it?

What can be done, in fact, is to make an analysis to discover how to improve the known/new rate, which is in itself only one of the main indicators, defined previously in Chapter 6, "Indicators Related to Knowledge Management".

Even though it is not at all simple, we need to try to plan our system in the best way possible so that we are able to arrive at this measurement.

To try to begin in the simplest and most practical way possible, we can try to analyze the occurrences of new, i.e., incidents attended to without there being any previous documentation. The challenge can be related to certain reasons:

- The universe (quantity) of incidents can be high.
- The incidents are probably related to several different areas of knowledge.
- It may be difficult to stratify information, i.e., generate some type of grouping to observe a certain trend, as it concerns abstract issues.

The fact that it is not a simple activity does not mean that we must not try.

Furthermore, it is a vital part of the process.

The KCS methodology suggests facing this challenge in four steps:

Step 1: definition of scope

Definition of the incident types, or incident groups, on which the work will be executed. It is also advisable to define a period of analysis and a percentage or number of incidents which will be taken as a sample. In this step the data which will be evaluated is also defined. I recommend looking for the balance between quantity and complexity of analysis of this data.

I also take the liberty of suggesting a score in accordance with the answers to the items, to record the result in a quantifiable value. This can be useful to compare the evolution of the system in periodic and cyclical analyses. You can change the values as you judge appropriate and can prefer to give greater or less weight to each item of the analysis.

In a first phase, we recommend using the data listed in Table 10.1. There is a spreadsheet suggested by KCS, with more information, which can be downloaded from the consortium site. In this spreadsheet a greater calculation of results is done. I am proposing here a particular format, more simplified, to determine these values.

Table 10.1. Recommended known x new analysis data.

Attributes of incidents and articles		
Incident code		
Incident title		
Linked article code		
Article title		
Article keywords		
Data analysis	**Suggested score**	**Remarks**
Incident with linked article?	Y: 3 N: 0	If the incident has any linked article
Linked article is correct?	Y: 3 N: -3	-Is the link done with the correct article? -An erroneous link annuls the positive value of having a link
Link created when creating incident	Y: 2 N: 0	If the link is created at the moment of creating the incident (there may be a link, but the article was created on-demand during assistance)
No link, but is there an appropriate article?	Y: -2 N: 0	Indication that there was a knowledge record which was not linked – in theory, it may not have been used, resulting in waste of time.
Advanced diagnosis required?	Y : it does not record any result	This is an indicator that very probably it was not possible to present a documented solution in an article, as the problem has not yet been well defined – this item, if marked as 'Yes', excludes the other analyses

Step 2: data collection

Generation of listing of incidents with the attributes to be analyzed, as defined as scope and as suggested in Table 10.1. Obtaining this type of listing obviously is no simple matter to be done without a suitable tool.

Step 3: analysis of incidents

This step is the most important and critical. It consists of analyzing the incidents and articles of the sample to evaluate their form, their content, indeed, to understand what the requirement refers to. It is necessary that this analysis has the participation of people with appropriate knowledge in the subject of the incidents. It is rather analytical work, which is why we insist that the sample must be limited. A very large volume of incidents to be analyzed can make the practical result unfeasible.

To execute the analysis, a good practice is to generate a spreadsheet with the attributes of incidents and articles in lines, together with the space to answer the analysis data. The data analysis columns can then be marked as 'Yes' or 'No', as per the conclusion regarding the respective evaluations. The answers 'Yes' and 'No' will result in a sum of points (as per suggestion of Table 10.1), which in turn can be added in the lines, resulting in a numerical score for a certain number of incidents.

The scoring system proposed is of the type 'the higher, the better'. The value in itself does not mean much as an absolute number, as it will depend upon the number of incidents pre-selected in the sample.

167

What is important is that this value is kept and that the next analysis is executed preferably with the same number of incidents. Thus, we shall have a comparative reference of trend indicating if there is any improvement in the system as a whole.

Step 4: identification and prioritization of opportunities for improvement

It is the step in which we mount an action plan, resulting from conclusions arrived at in the previous step. We are going to enter into greater detail regarding this analysis further on, in a topic related to monthly procedures during the operation of the system (15.2).

10.2. Sampling audit of contents

Another type of check which can be extremely desirable concerns the contents of the articles themselves, examining the adherence to standards established regarding the clarity of writing, objectivity and efficiency of summarizing, for example.

An audit of this type must be based exclusively upon the standards established for comparison with what has been recorded, avoiding any subjective personal interpretations.

During our planning, in the chapter concerning knowledge base structuring we defined our good documentation practices (7.3), and that is what must be used in the audit.

The process is identical to audits of quality management systems or similar ones. A periodicity is defined for the audits, which are scheduled and, as per scheduling, executed. In the end, a report must be produced with the observations and indications made by the auditor.

If your company has an audit system already implemented, aim to insert a specific item about article documentation quality.

Another alternative is that the area manager executes this sampling analysis in periods not scheduled, with follow-up in the day-to-day of the operation.

Whatever the checking method may be, I recommend that a formalization of the observations is generated, which will have an educational purpose, as it will aid in indicating flaws or inappropriate practices.

A knowledge management indicator can also be defined related to this number of observations. The access to these formalized observations can also aid in training new people, as an example and as guidance.

Important note

It is advisable that at the start of the operation of the system the periodicity of the sampling audits is weekly. We cannot waste the opportunity of maintaining the total focus on the constant observation of the system, which is also important for showing people the continuous involvement in the process.

Table 10.2. Suggestion of formalization of observations related to audit of contents

AUDIT REPORT		
Audit date:		Auditor:
Findings		
Article	**Author**	**Remarks**

11. Definition of Criteria of Incentive and Acknowledgement

We have here the planning of the knowledge management system almost all concluded. The last point that we are going to deal with – last, but by no means less important – is the question of people, more precisely the possible ways of encouraging them to be committed to the system.

From the point of view of KCS, there are two main motivating factors: alignment with the objectives and sense of fulfillment and acknowledgement.

I believe that these really are important factors to which we must dedicate time for planning and implementation. I prefer not to look here at the financial issue directly related to remuneration, as it extrapolates the scope of implementation of a system. Clearly in a company where all the people are lacking in motivation for this reason it may be more difficult to look at other motivational issues. Or not...

Once again, I am going to ask the reader's permission to leave the guidebook a little aside and follow a slightly adapted path. Even because the cultural realities are a little different, and KCS is all oriented towards the reality of companies of the consortium.

11.1. Alignment with objectives

Although my area of specialization is not human resources, I believe, in fact, that people of any area are motivated when they work with common objectives and really understand how these objectives are aligned with the business and goals of the organization. People also need to understand how they contribute to these objectives.

Therefore, it is essential that the area has then clearly defined its objectives, and that the latter are aligned with the organizational objectives. The great majority of companies have strategic planning. It is necessary to show people how their area, their process, us aligned with the strategic objectives of the company. In some way, the goals achieved in a certain area must contribute to the greater goals of the company, in the value chain.

The recommendation is that the indicators which are defined, and their goals, are clearly explained and presented in a manner aligned with the business objectives.

This, in theory, makes people motivated to attain them.

Returning to the issue of financial reward, a good suggestion for joining this alignment together with obtaining reward is through some deferred profit sharing programs (DPSP), which are rather well known. As these programs follow certain regulations and require formal and legalized approval in agreements, it is not something which you implement overnight. But, at the same time, the knowledge management system itself begins by planning and a pilot phase, which takes some time.

So, the suggestion is to align knowledge management indicators already validated, when you have them, to the indices which compose the profit distribution conditions and starters. This is an unquestionable way that the company acknowledges the system, values it and, at the same time, gives coworkers the possibility of financial reward with results aligned with the objectives.

11.2. Sense of fulfillment and acknowledgement

This item is of fundamental importance, on the personal side and also because it impacts on the previous item. As it is of a personal sphere, it is very subjective. Each person can feel fulfilled in a different way. Each person can experience different sensations for the same type of acknowledgement, informal or formal.

Generally speaking, we can think that the sense of fulfillment occurs upon attaining an objective, upon achieving something which was proposed – always linked to the indicators, their goals and the alignment thereof with the business objectives.

And acknowledgement? What exactly makes people feel acknowledged?

A good practice which can be adopted so that both people's objectives and attributions are clear is to update the formal descriptions of job title and their responsibilities with HR, reflecting profile requirements and obligations related to the knowledge management system.

In the cases of companies which have formal evaluation of employees performance, theoretically there already exists an established acknowledgement system. These attributions related to knowledge management would be formally considered in employee evaluation and acknowledgement. These responsibilities, ideally, can be placed together with clauses of achieving individual and group goals. Thus, the effort and personal success will be more complete if all the group is successful.

12. Final Preparations for the Implementation

With the planning practically ready and having formalized the definitions required, we can now move on to the last preparations required before the entry of the system into production, the so called go-live.

These preparations concern two groups of activities. We need to pay attention to the documentation of our system and the training of the people who will take part in the process; next, we must focus upon the proactive generation of knowledge for which we have already detected gaps and of which the known flaws need handling.

12.1. Documentation and training

It is worth bearing in mind that we involve several people in the planning, and it is necessary to document the system as a whole. We also need to establish how the people will be trained, either the start training before the implementation for the current team, or also for new coworkers who may come to be part of the team in the future. It is no use beginning to run our system with all those involved in the current team trained and, in the case of turnover, not execute transmission to the new components of the group.

Each organization has its practices of documentation of procedures and instructions.

You can, obviously, use the model which is most adapted to your company. Anyway, and whatever your documentation format, certain elements cannot fail to exist.

I recommend, therefore, that you have at least the following elements defined and with access known by everyone:

- Documentation of your support process, with the knowledge matrix, knowledge gaps and tacit knowledge by responsibility.
- Training material for people involved in assistance:
  - Engagement training with basic concepts of knowledge management and KCS.
  - Training about the operation, the day-to-day. Above all it involves training in the tool to be used, its functions, indeed, how to operate the system. How to create and review articles, for example.
- Indicators oriented towards business and related to knowledge management.
  - It is excellent that we have indicators, but where will they be published?
  - How will they be accessed by people?
  - It is absolutely essential that everybody understands all the indicators, their meaning and their goals,
- Instructions manual concerning the structuring of the knowledge base and the use of the system.
- Access to the data and results of 'known x new' analyses.
- Access to audit findings.
- Access to all action plans.

With this material ready, it remains to execute the final training and schedule the start date.

> Although so far the path seems laborious, the greatest challenge is yet to come: when the system begins to run.

The leader responsible for the direct follow-up shall be disposed, dedicate time and above all be persistent. It is very likely that people's commitment level oscillates, for several reasons. And it is exactly in the situations of "slackening" that the leader's persistence is required to orientate, request, correct and adjust.

12.2. Proactive creation of knowledge

In the long path traveled so far, during the knowledge mapping phase, we detected certain knowledge gaps which were mapped during the analysis of the process and the assets. If our analysis was correct, then this information and this knowledge have value and are necessary.

The moment has arrived for us to start preparing these contents, or these articles. We need to assign to the respective specialists in the subjects the responsibility for preparing the articles, so that the system already begins to run with the greatest quantity possible of these information gaps filled.

Besides these knowledge gaps, information can be listed for end users, which should also be done before the start of the operations.

Finally, knowledge requirements may have been detected regarding account profiles and customer configurations, which must also be dealt with at this point.

Some of the items mentioned may be complex to prepare, which takes up a lot of time. It is up to you to analyze and take the decision between awaiting the finishing of these procedures or beginning to run the system even without concluding them.

In my opinion, having an action plan clearly defined, we can begin to run the system even without all the planning items finished. Certain benefits will already be noted with the updates of content on demand.

13. Reflections Regarding Return on Investment (ROI)

Now we are going to look at an issue as important as it is complex and polemical.

Will it be possible to measure the return on investment in the implementation of a knowledge management system in support services?

There are people longing to find this nirvana, who would love to arrive at a direct result which allowed them to place in a column the total of expenses, in the form of investments and costs, and on the other side a direct financial return, representing a financial balance, preferably a positive one.

Before proceeding, I want to remind you that this quest is very common in other service areas, as assistance itself, whether in service desk, help desk or assistance to users or consumers.

In answer to the fundamental question: it can even be possible, depending upon the type of business and its size.

It can be possible, but it is not simple. And it is not easy.

And the reason is as follows: there are no direct revenues related to assistance – except, clearly, in cases where the end activity is selling services related to assistance, as in certain support contracts with revenue related to support.

A concept universally accepted for measuring return is related to productivity, which means, in services, rendering more services with the same resources, or rendering the same volume of services with fewer resources.

We can begin reflecting about the direct productivity gains which we can obtain in assistance services with the appropriate adoption of knowledge management practices.

What are these supposed gains? Invariably they are related to rendering services with greater efficacy, which can mean doing it in less time.

Resolving incidents or requisitions in less time, it is possible to respond to more incidents or requisitions with the same number of people. We can also imagine that gains in productivity will occur increasing the number of solutions resolved at the first assistance level, avoiding involving human resources of the more specialized and less available scheduling levels.

It is worth noting that we are scoring items related directly to productivity, in order to try to achieve a financial quantification. Obviously, there are other benefits, already widely discussed, related to the perception of quality of the services and other benefits of knowledge management.

I, personally, have always considered very relative all the studies about ROI and the (in)famous total cost of property – TCO, as they are always based upon rather abstract or case study conditional premises. But, on the other hand, it is clear that, as an exercise and as a reference, these studies are valid, or, in the worst case, are better than not having studied anything.

In our case of support services, the greatest likelihood of success in the calculation of financial return is directly related to the size of the operation, whether in number of assistances or in number of agents. With small teams or a relatively small absolute number of agents, we do not have a scale to quantify satisfactorily financial gains arising from the optimization of the assistance times. The reasoning continues to be simple: an average reduction in assistance time, multiplied by a moderate number of issues, multiplied by a moderate number of agents, multiplied by the cost/time of the agents, can represent something not so financially relevant. To the extent that any one of these variables increases a lot, or they all do, the impact measured can be greater.

Anyway, and whatever may be size in your organization, it is clear that the average assistance time must be measured, comparing values obtained with the implementation of knowledge management related to the baseline, taken before implementing the system – see Chapter 6, "Review and Definition of Monitoring Items".

We are going to simulate, in the following table, a hypothetical calculation to illustrate an estimated time reduction. Perhaps it is not very significant to consider the figures of 20 minutes and 15 minutes, respectively. More important is the average reduction of 5 minutes per assistance.

Table 13.1. Simulation of calculation of gain in productivity

Number of demands /month	AAT before implement. of Knowledge Management	AAT after implement. of Knowledge Management	Total time reduced
800	20	15	(20-15)*800 = 4000 minutes **66,6 hs**

AAT stands for Average Assistance Time: average time spent by agents per issue

For many people, it can seem very obvious now to study the average cost/hour of the assistance people and multiply it by the number of hours saved.

This is where I begin to disagree partially with the ROI calculations which we see around.

Let us say that this multiplication is done and one arrives at a certain amount, for example, USD 3,000.00. What then? How are we going to reduce these three thousand dollars of cost of staff equivalent to 66 hours in a month? Unless the objective is, on a larger scale, to reduce people, this calculation is not totally justified.

So, I prefer to analyze it from another point of view: what can be produced more with these 66 hours which "became available". Thus, again, we can fall into subjective concepts – I repeat, unless it is a support company which executes assistance and charges by the hour. In this case, and only in this case, a potential gain of 66 hours more to be invoiced was obtained.

14. Summary – 40 Planning Items

We are arriving at the end of the planning of our knowledge management system.

To facilitate the follow-up of the implementation and execution of all the suggestions proposed, we present a checklist encompassing all the activities and actions looked at so far.

It may be interesting for you to use this table in the form of a project, with stages and phases, to be able thereby to have greater control over the implementation, even more so if you are not involved personally in all of them. This will allow you to delegate certain activities and even so maintain control over their progress.

Remember, once again, that the concepts are simple, but being successful in the implementation may not be. The quantity of items, 40, in itself only gives more clearly the idea of the volume of work involved.

Clearly, you can opt to shorten the path, not following all the steps.

This does not mean that you will not manage to have a result. I believe, however, that all the items presented and justified have sense and relevance to achieve the objective.

Table 14.1. Forty planning items

Process aproach		
	1	Mapping and documentation of activities of the help desk or customer care process
	2	For each process activity, identify and document 'moments of truth'
	3	For each process activity, identify and document critical points
	4	For each process activity, identify and document handoffs
	5	Definition of process and KM key point indicators

Prepare for deploy		
	6	Obtain formal support of C-level executive
	7	Identify leaders to take part of the project
	8	Identify area and process for pilot program
	9	Prepare and execute executive presentation for engagement
	10	Schedule and execute planning meetings

Information and knowledge assets		
	11	For each process activity, identify and document required information and required knowledge

	12	For each process activity, identify and document tacit information and tacit knowledge
	13	For each process activity, identify and document explicit information and explicit knowledge
	14	Create matrices of explicit and tacit knowledge
	15	Create an 'explicit knowledge gap' listing
	16	Identify and document knowledge that is suitable to be collected during execution of process
	17	Identify and define information to be made available to end users or clients, including 'top 10' if possible
	18	Identify and define knowledge management key point indicators

Knowledge base design		
	19	Definition of types of articles
	20	Definition of information attributes
	21	Definition of 'Good Documentation Practices'
	22	Definition of storage structure
	23	Definition of a model for publishing and updating content
	24	Assignemnt of Responsibilities
	25	Definition of information attributes and gathering of account profiles
	26	Definition of information attributes and gathering of client configuration data

'Known x new' sampling analysis		
	27	Scope definition
	28	Definition of data to be analyzed when collected
	29	Definition of how collection is to be made

Audit of contents		
	30	Definition of expected audit findings
	31	Definition of auditors
	32	Definition of periodicity and planning of audits
	33	Execution of audits, weekly if possible

Criteria for reward and recognition		
	34	Define alignment of reward and recognition practices to corporate polices – responsibilities on knowledge management

Final preps		
	35	Instructions manual on operations, general structure and utilization
	36	Preparation of material for employee's training
	37	Provide employee's training

	38	Preparation and publication of knowledge listed as 'knowledge gap'
	39	Preparation and publication of knowledge to be made available to end-users and clients
	40	Preparation and publication of knowledge related to account profiles and client configuration

15. Knowledge Management System Operation

You and the other people involved in the implementation of knowledge management in your company have probably worked hard so far. If you are beginning to operate your system, then your plan, in a more or less detailed level, in some way was done.

This is excellent. Congratulations.

It is relevant to put in perspective the point where we started and where we are.

Probably many who were interested by this book had little or no knowledge in the area; arriving here, we have already managed to learn many new concepts and think about our business, planning how to implement a knowledge management system focused upon our reality, our business, our process.

All the work developed so far corresponds to the "P" of the famous PDCA. Henceforth, we are going to deal with the remainder of the cycle, including the execution itself (D), check (C) and the general analysis of the performance of our system, where we shall be able to execute actions of correction or improvement (A).

15.1. Following up the day-to-day

As soon as your system begins to operate, ideally you should adopt a personalized follow-up posture. This can and must be done by the person assuming the role of mentor. In the first days, especially, the mentor is expected to be directly with

187

the people, at their side, resolving doubts and aiding to achieve what was proposed: creating and updating knowledge to the extent that the assistance occurs.

It cannot be expected that at the start everything functions perfectly in an automatic manner. They may be, and certainly there will be, forgetfulness, mistakes and doubts.

What is important, at the start, is to maintain focused upon the operation and be ready to be helpful to aid in the issues which arise.

During the first months it is highly advisable that the audits sampling contents are executed weekly, if not daily.

It is also advisable to plan quick moments of weekly review in group, when ideally everybody takes part. Clearly, as we have already mentioned it is not possible to stop support entirely, which is a complicating fact. One should at least try to manage to have a weekly moment, even if only for 10 or 15 minutes, to speak about the difficulties found, lessons learnt and where the people in the group can present their perceptions. Many usually call moments such as these stand-up meetings, occasions of really brief and objective exchanges.

15.2. Monthly procedures

If some of the recommendations mentioned are desirable, there are fundamental and mandatory activities, under penalty of jeopardizing the continuity of the system. That is right, **they are so important that they can represent the difference between success or lack of success of the system as a whole.** The periodicity must be monthly, so ideally they are always executed at the start of the month following the one of the analysis. They are as follows:

188

15.2.1. Formal known x new analysis

It is worth bearing in mind that, during the planning, the four steps recommended for the 'known x new' analysis were presented. The first step corresponds to the definition of scope, i.e., which types of demand will be analyzed. All the following steps correspond to the execution of activities, what must be done now that the system is operational.

The procedure which we need to execute, initially, is to generate the listing of the demands, whether they are incidents or requisitions, which are appropriate to the scope determined.

Next, we must start the analysis, using the spreadsheet which we defined in the planning phase; to the extent that the data is checked, it is scored and we determine a numerical value for a specified number of demands.

This value is not so important in itself, but for comparison over time, month after month, giving an indication of trend of possible improvement of the system as a whole – after all, theoretically what is wanted is to have the maximum possible demands attended to with defined and efficient tacit documentation.

The individual analysis of demands and their articles is fundamental to have a sample of the general quality and efficacy of the process. Individually, however, it can be difficult to define correction or adjustment actions, mainly due to a possible high data volume. On the other hand, if the scope has been defined with a very low volume of demands, it may have little significance related to the world of sampling.

The main challenge, therefore, during the execution of the system, is to analyze the data collected and find some type of standard, or correlation, which allows adjustment or corrective actions to be generated which are relevant to a common group of causes. It is something complex, said to be passing, mainly as it is subjective. It is subjective even for defining formally what type of correlation is sought. With the knowledge of business and process, and with time, certain trends can become clear and indicate these standards.

Certain examples of conclusions which could possibly be observed:

- For a certain type of incident, related to a certain area of knowledge, it is perceived that the occurrence of "nonexistent articles" is greater.
- An above average number of linked articles which are not appropriate is observed for a group of agents.
- A determined group of people stands out due to the creation of articles during assistance, but these articles could be better worded regarding clarity and synthesis.

We can have several others, but with the examples mentioned it is already possible to have an idea, however superficial it may be, about what is sought.

If a type of pattern is found, it is the moment to start correction or adjustment actions. It does not need to be complex or difficult to control, but also it is not good to leave these actions totally informal.

I recommend at least that actions are generated with assignment and due dates, that they are formalized and that they are checked in the next cycle, in the following month.

A simple example with actions is presented in the table below.

Table 15.1. Adjustment actions arising from known x new analysis

Analysis date:		
What	When	When
Analyze documentation which could be created proactively for incidents of type 'X'		
Create articles referring to the previous analysis		
Recycling training concerning the good practices of documentation guide for groups X and Y		

15.2.2. Generation, analysis and publication of indicators

A basic assumption of quality systems applies here. **Processes and indicators are of no use if they are not used for some purpose.**

Indicators only make sense if they are periodically collected, documented, analyzed, have correction actions and are published.

Without this, they tend to become a total waste of time and resources.

For the time being, in our monthly analysis, we are going to be concerned with the indicators related to knowledge management. Those indicators which we defined in the planning phase must first be collected and documented. Ideally they should be documented clearly, so that a quick reading allows the understanding of that which was measured. No abbreviated codes or very codified representations.

Each indicator defined has, after collected and documented, its measurement values.

The objective is to establish a comparative reference over time. And this is what must be analyzed. The analysis can be simple and informal, provided that it is recorded. We can answer simple questions, as the following ones, for example, supposing that the indicators show these trends:

- Why is the absolute number of articles created falling?
- Why did the known x new rate fall drastically?
- Why did some people manage to create a lot more articles than the other in the group?

Typically, an analysis of indicators also includes the question of achievement or not of goals. I would like to remind you that we may have opted to define goals or not – we discussed this in planning, in the chapter about the indicators related to knowledge management.

If in your organization you have defined goals, it is highly advisable to make an analysis regarding the possible non-fulfillment thereof, for each indicator, specifying the suspected causes.

So far, we have collected, documented and analyzed indicators. In many cases we need to generate correction or adjustment actions. This can be clearly specified by the indicator trend, whether a subtle trend or an exception, where a more striking anomaly is observed. The same observation made concerning the known x new analysis is also valid here. It is necessary to strike the right balance between generating actions indiscriminately, for everything, and not generating adjustment actions which are important.

As a rule, an action is generated for each and any critical result observed, the sensitivity and reality of each organization being valid in this case. Apart from critical occurrences, a criterion can be established to define which cases generate action, which, albeit simplistic, is better than not having any criterion.

A practice suggested is related to the observation of trend. **When results of indicators show a trend of stagnating to falling for, let us say, three months consecutively, it may be a good idea to generate an action of investigation and adjustment**.

If you have goals established, a certain number of periods without a goal achieved is an indication that something needs to be investigated.

The actions can be generated in the same manner as suggested in the previous topic; what is important is to have their execution followed up at each analysis – always checking actions generated in the previous analysis.

Regarding the indicators, there still lacks one of the fundamental parts which we mentioned at the start of this chapter: their availability. Publish your indicators and analysis in the most formal manner possible. Avoid only communicating that the month's indicators are published in a certain network folder, or on the portal of the intranet; often we commit this error. We work in all the system with dedication and energy, but we fail in publishing and, mainly, in ensuring that everybody is aware of and understands the results of the indicators.

As far as possible, present them highlighted and in an organized manner. Ideally it would be in person, gathering together the people for a presentation, which can be brief, lasting about 15 minutes. If it is not possible, at least prepare an organized presentation document easy to understand.

15.3. Critical analysis of the system

A critical analysis of the system is an activity of a more strategic than operational approach.

It concerns analyzing how the system is functioning, from a more managerial and executive point of view. Ideally there is the participation of at least one top executive.

A critical analysis serves to evaluate "if it is worth the trouble, or what we are gaining with this, or also what we need to change for it to be worth the effort and obtain some benefit".

Thus, the critical analysis must look at the indicators oriented towards business – which were defined at the start of the planning.

Do you remember, dear reader, that we dealt with this issue?

I mentioned that it is no use only looking at intrinsic indicators of KM, that we also have to look at the result for process. For example, what is the use having all the indicators related to knowledge management positive if the general perception for customers has not changed?

This is the moment for this type of analysis, even for reflection. It is also the appropriate moment to analyze the allocation of resources and possible new requirement. A good cycle which can be recommended for these analyses is every three months.

It may seem rather too obvious to mention the importance of and suggest an activity like this. But it is not. First, because the obvious can be made relative, depending upon the perspective and responsibilities of each one. Secondly, because it is essential that you, as authority for implementation of knowledge management, leave this "obvious" arranged with top management so that there is participation and commitment – you shall have obtained the support of a top executive in the stage of defining responsibilities, way back, in the planning.

Leave it clear to the top management supporter, therefore, that this activity shall occur every three months, seeking to make him/her jointly responsible for the success of the knowledge management system.

Next, we make a minimum relevant suggestion for these meetings. Try to leave the analyses documented for formalization and follow-up.

Suggestion of agenda for critical analysis meeting of the knowledge management system

- Analysis of indicators oriented towards process: review of the indicators, follow-up of the evolution.
- Succinct presentation of indicators related to knowledge management: as they are operational, a short presentation is sufficient, focusing upon positive or negative points.
- Conclusions concerning indicators (succinct, documented in a few phrases).
- General analysis of the system: conclusions, in a few objective phrases.
- Actions to be taken (if they exist).

16. Conclusion

Whenever I finish reading any technical book, I usually ask myself at least three questions, which obviously I try to answer.

I ask myself:

- Am I ending the reading of this book knowing more about the subject than when I began?
- Did the content aid me in any way with what I intended?
- Did I have a new idea?

I hope that you, reader, can answer positively to one or more questions.

This would have made it worth the trouble.

As a final message, from someone who to a certain extent got carried away with the issue, I should like to say that the subject is not exhausted by what has been seen.

Much content and many ideas are produced. If you are interested in implementing knowledge management in your company, on a greater or smaller scale, you already have knowledge and a starting point.

I'd like to hear from you. For comments or suggestions please reach me at jst999@gmail.com.

Good luck!

Bibliographic References

APQC. APQC Knowledge Map and Process Map Overview. Technical article. Oct.2, 2009

ATKINSON, R.; CUSTY, J.; JOSLIN, Rick. Synergies Between ITIL® and Knowledge-Centered Support. Available at: <https://www.axelos.com/case-studies-and-white-papers/synergies-between-itil-knowledge-centered-support>. Access on: Sep 29, 2015.

BELLINGER, G. Knowledge Management: emerging perspectives. 2004. Available at: <http://systems-thinking.org/kmgmt/kmgmt.htm>. Access on: Sep 29, 2015.

BOSTON KM FORUM. Knowledge Mapping. PowerPoint presentation. 2007.

CHOO, C. W. The Knowing Organization: how organizations use information for construct meaning, create knowledge and make decisions. New York: Oxford Press, 1998.

CONSORTIUM FOR SERVICE INNOVATION. KCS Adoption Guide.

CONSORTIUM FOR SERVICE INNOVATION. KCS Practices Guide.

DALKIR, K. Knowledge Management in Theory and Practice. Burlington, MA: Elsevier, 2005.

KM KNOWLEDGE MANAGEMENT. Knowledge Conversion and the Knowledge Spiral. Mar. 1st, 2011. Available at: <www.skyrme.com/kmbasics/kspiral.htm>. Access on: Sep 29, 2015.

KNOWLEDGE RESEARCH INSTITUTE and other sources. Knowledge Management Glossary. Available at:

<http://www.krii.com/downloads/KM_glossary.pdf>. Access on: Sep 29, 2015.

KNOWLEDGE RESEARCH INSTITUTE. Case Stories and Vignettes from Many Sources. Available at: <http://www.krii.com/downloads/100_KM_case_stories.pdf>. Access on: Sep 29, 2015.

NONAKA, I.; TAKEUCHI, H. The Knowledge-creating Company: How Japanese Companies Create the Dynamics of Innovation. Oxford Press, 1995.

NORTON, D. P.; KAPLAN, R. S. Kaplan e Norton na Practica. Rio de Janeiro: Campus, 2004.

SIMKOVITS, H. Discipline of Market Leaders: three fundamental business strategies – from "The Discipline of Market Leaders" by Treacy and Wiersema. Business Wisdom

Web Portal. Available at: <http://www.business-wisdom.com/articles/ArtclDisciplineOfMarket.html>. Access on: Sep 29, 2015.

STATDLOBER, J. Help-desk e SAC com Qualidade. Rio de Janeiro: Brasport, 2006.

URIARTE JR., F. A. Introduction to Knowledge Management. Jakarta: ASEAN Foundation, 2008.

WIIG, K. M. Knowledge Management 20 years after... The evolution and increasing significance of Knowledge Management. Fifth European Conference on Knowledge Management, Paris, 2004.

WIIG, K. M. Knowledge Management for the Competitive Enterprise. Arlington, TX: Knowledge Research Institute, 2009.

WIIG, K. M. Successful Knowledge Management: does it exist? European American Business Journal, Aug. 1999.

WILSON, T. D. The nonsense of 'knowledge management'. Information Research, vol. 8, n. 1, Oct. 2002. Available at: <http://www.informationr.net/ir/8-1/paper144.html>. Access on: Sep 29, 2015.

About the author

Juliano Statdlober has multidisciplinary knowledge and experience which encompass technology and management. Bachelor's Degree in Economic Sciences and Postgraduate in IT Governance, he has been working in Information Technology since 1983, with knowledge and expertise including COBIT, ITIL, BPM, KM, project management and quality management systems. He has wide professional experience in service management and business process management. An entrepreneur, he performs as CTO in the company Qualitor Software, of which he is founding partner and responsible for the Software Development and Technology area. His first book published to the Brazilian market is about Quality Management related to help desk and customer care. This second book, about knowledge management for help desk and customer care is published as an international edition.

Printed in Great Britain
by Amazon

41896578R00121